COLLINS'
PHRASE BOOKS

COLLINS'
PHRASE BOOKS
FRENCH: GERMAN: ITALIAN:
SPANISH

INSTANTANEOUS IN USE

The complete Index, practical subdivision of Subjects, and clear bold type, ensure that the required phrases are found immediately.

EASILY UNDERSTOOD

The clear and accurate pronunciation of every word may be read simply as English syllables, and the use of confusing symbols is avoided.

UP-TO-DATE

The most modern requirements of travellers on the Continent are fully dealt with, including Air Travel, Motoring, etc.

ACCURATE

The sentences are expressed in the latest idioms by experts in both languages, while the information included has been officially checked.

PRACTICAL

The practical choice of sentences, the introductory advice and the many hints on difficulties are invaluable to tourists and business men alike.

COLLINS' PHRASE BOOKS

ITALIAN

Edited by
ISOPEL MAY, B.A., Ph.D.

COLLINS
LONDON AND GLASGOW

GENERAL EDITOR: G. F. MAINE

First Published, 1936
New Edition, 1951
Reprinted, 1953
   ,,   1954
Revised, 1955
Reprinted, 1956

Printed in Great Britain by
COLLINS CLEAR-TYPE PRESS

CONTENTS

CONTENTS

NOTE ON SCHEME OF PRONUNCIATION

The pronunciations given should be read simply as English syllables, with the stress placed on the syllable immediately before the accent mark ('). This will ensure that the sentences are read in correct Italian ; the following notes may help visitors to pronounce new words.

In Italian :

A is pronounced like English *a* in *far*.

E is pronounced like English *a* in *fate*.

I is pronounced like English *ee* in *feet*.

O is pronounced roughly like English *o* in *oh* !

U is pronounced like English *oo* in *boot*.

C before *a*, *o* and *u* and CH before *e* and *i* has the sound of English *K*.

C before *e* and *i* has the sound of English *ch* in *church*.

SC before *e* and *i* has the sound of English *sh* in *bush*.

G before *a*, *o* and *u* is pronounced hard (like English *get*).

G before *e* and *i* is pronounced like English *J*.

H is always mute.

R should always be pronounced distinctly.

Z has two sounds, which may be represented by *dz*, *ts*.

When double consonants are found, both should be pronounced distinctly.

In giving the pronunciation, the words have been split into syllables, but they should of course be pronounced without pauses between the syllables.

INTRODUCTION

ROUTES TO ITALY.—The more important travel routes from Continental countries to Italy are :

By Rail :

    From *France :* Nice—Ventimiglia—Genoa (or Ventimiglia—Breil—Turin).

    Paris—Dijon—Modane—Turin.

    From *Switzerland :* Bâle—Berne—Brigue (or Lausanne—Brigue)—Domodossola—Milan.

    Bâle—Lucerne—Bellinzona—Chiasso—Milan.

    Lucerne—Bellinzona—Luino—Milan (or Turin).

    From *Austria :* Innsbruck—Brennero—Verona. Vienna—Tarvisio—Udine—Venice.

    From *Yugoslavia :* Ljubljana—Poggio Reale— Trieste—Venice.

By Air :

    London—Paris—Milan ; London—Paris—Rome. Brussels—Milan ; Madrid—Rome.

PASSPORTS.—Passports (endorsed for Italy, France and Switzerland) are necessary, but no consular visa is required for British subjects for travelling to the above countries. The passport should always be carried as an identification paper together with the declaration of sojourn (see below, Police Regulations, page 11).

CUSTOMS.—On express trains luggage is examined in the compartments ; in all other cases the luggage must be taken to the customs office. Passengers are required to attend personally to the customs formalities at the frontier, but luggage registered to the more important

Italian towns can be cleared on arrival at the destination.
Every article is dutiable in Italy, but bona fide personal
effects intended for the use of the traveller are exempt.
Foodstuffs, beverages and tobacco are not regarded as
personal effects and are therefore exempted only for such
small quantities as may be required by the traveller for
actual use on the train, having regard to the duration of
the journey. In any case, any amount of tobacco imported
should be declared.

TIME-TABLES (L'orario, *lor-rah'ree-oh*).—Time in Italy
and Switzerland is based on the Central European Time,
which is one hour in advance of Greenwich Time and
corresponds to " Summer Time " in Great Britain and
France. Times are given according to the 24-hour system.
Names of stations are frequently given in one order only,
with times printed on both sides and marked by arrows
to show the direction of the trains, thus :

10.00	Chambéry	..	arr.	^	1.20
11.25	Modane	..	part.		23.45
12.20	,,	..	arr.		23.00
14.40	Torino, P.N.	..	part.		20.40

The best time-table is the *Orario Generale Pozzo*
(350 *liras*), showing railway, tram, bus, boat and air
services for the whole of Italy. Other time-tables, handier
and quite inexpensive, cover only a part of the country.

TRAINS.—Trains in Italy are of several types :

Rapidi (rah'pee-dee) are special fast trains (first and
second class) between two main towns, having no inter-
mediate stop. An extra charge is made for travelling on
these trains. On the Milan-Rome-Naples line these
trains are called *elettrotreni* (ay-let-troh-tray'nee).

Automotrici Rapidi (ow-toh-moh-tree'chee rah'pee-dee)
are fast streamlined Diesel-engined trains with two coaches
only containing first class and dining accommodation.

Littorine (leet-tor-ree'nay) are Diesel-engined coaches,
generally only second class, though a few have second
and third, which are used for short distances.

Direttissimi (dee-ret-teess'see-mee) (first and second class, or first, second and third class) are express trains. Third-class travellers for *short* sections are excluded.

Diretti (dee-ret'tee) (first, second and third class) are slower express trains.

Accelerati (ahch-chay-lay-rah'tee), *Omnibus* (om'nee-bouss) and *Misti* (mee'stee) are slow trains (generally second and third class only), the last two stop at all stations.

LUGGAGE.—Hand luggage taken by travellers into the compartment may not exceed 20 kgs. (or 44 lbs.) nor take the place on the rack intended for other travellers' luggage. Any quantity in excess is charged at registered luggage rates (in addition to a small surtax) and the excess luggage is removed, when deemed necessary, to the luggage van. There is no free allowance for registered luggage.

AIR TRAVEL.—There are many air services in Italy connecting the capital daily with the principal Italian towns, as well as with neighbouring countries. There is a free allowance for luggage up to 15 kgs. (33 lbs.). Cameras must be declared in order that they may be sealed and kept by the personnel of the plane during the flight.

POLICE REGULATIONS; DECLARATION OF SOJOURN [Dichiarazione di soggiorno (dee-kee-ah-raht-see-oh'nay dee sod-jorr'noh)].—Foreigners must, within three days from their arrival in Italy, register with the police (see page 51) and obtain a paper signed by the Commissioner of Police, which they should always carry with them. Travellers staying at hotels can ask the hotel-keeper to attend to this formality, but the responsibility for non-compliance with the law rests upon the travellers.

USE OF CAMERAS, MAPS, ETC.—Within the " frontier zone " as defined by special laws, which extends to several miles from the actual frontier-line, it is forbidden to take photographs or make drawings, and to use large-scale maps. Cameras can be carried in transit by road or rail, if declared at the customs office (where they are sealed) or if contained in trunks, other than hand luggage.

Painters and amateur photographers can apply for a special permit to the Command of the Military Division.

In addition to the above, it is forbidden throughout the country to take photographs or make drawings of buildings and works of a military character, or connected with national defence. The prohibited zone was marked in the past with stones and notice-boards, which are now being gradually replaced by the Touring Club Italiano with conspicuous metal boards reading : *Divieto di eseguire fotografie e rilievi* (dee-vee-ay'toh dee ay-zay-gwee'ray foh-toh-grah-fee'ay ay ree-lee-ay'vee):" Taking photographs or making maps is strictly forbidden :"

MOUNTAINEERING.—Tourists walking across the Alps are warned that it is forbidden to cross the Italian frontier except by authorised passes (*valichi di frontiera aperti al transito con passaporto*) where there exist police posts. Information as to the passes available for transit can be obtained locally. Tourists making excursions in the Alpine zone (on the Italian side) close to the frontier border must be in possession either of a *carta di turismo alpino* or of an endorsement to the same effect on their passport, which is obtained from the local police authorities. The carrying of arms without licence (including sporting or boy scout's knives) is liable to heavy penalty. Pocket knives with a blade not exceeding $2\frac{3}{8}$ in., if fitted to a handle less than 3 in. long, are allowed.

MEALS.—Meals comprise *prima colazione* or breakfast (coffee and milk, or chocolate, roll and butter, and biscuits), *colazione* or lunch, and *pranzo* or dinner. Lunch and dinner can be had at restaurants and *trattorie* (restaurants of a popular character. Some of them, however, are famous for their specialities and are frequented by connoisseurs). In the main towns and all resorts frequented by foreigners (the Lakes, the Riviera, etc.) there are " tea shops " or " Tea Rooms," as well as first-rate *pasticcerie-confetterie* or cake shops where tea is served.

TIPPING.—Tips have been nominally abolished, being almost everywhere replaced by the *percentuale di servizio*

(12 per cent in cafés and restaurants, and from 15 per cent to 18 per cent in hotels). It is advisable always to inquire whether service is included, but even if included waiters expect clients to " round up " the amount of the bill. In some places, the staff is forbidden to accept tips.

TOURISTS' TAX.—In all the large towns and places of resort, bills of hotels and pensions are increased by a tax [*tassa di soggiorno* (tahs'sah dee sod-jorr'noh)], which varies according to the class of hotel or pension. At present the hotel tax is . 60 liras per day in luxury hotels, 50 liras in first-class ones, 40 liras in second-class, 25 liras in third-class, 10 liras in fourth-class and 5 liras in the so-called *Locande* (loh-kahn'day). In first, second and third-class pensions the tax is 40, 25 and 10 liras respectively. For visitors making a longer stay these taxes are only charged for *one* month out of *three*. This tax is levied by means of stamps affixed to the bill in addition to the receipt stamp.

AMUSEMENTS.—In the more important towns there is a good opera season from December to April. Small seasons in summer are generally of a distinctly lower standard. The season for plays extends from September to June, and English plays translated into Italian can often be seen.

FORMS OF ADDRESS.—When addressing strangers, it is customary to preface any remark with *scusi* (skoo'zee), i.e. excuse me. Married ladies are addressed as *Signora* (seen-yor'ah) ; *Signorina* (seen-yor-ree'nah) is used in addressing unmarried young ladies.

GENERAL ADVICE.—In conversation with strangers one should avoid politics and abstain from general criticism.

TRAVELLING IN SWITZERLAND.—Italian is one of the three official languages of the Swiss Federal Government, and is spoken in the Canton Ticino (Bellinzona, Locarno, Lugano) as well as in some parts of the Cantone dei

Grigioni or Grisons. The difficulty of the language for an Englishman does not arise, however, in Switzerland, as throughout the country hotel staffs and railway officials can speak English. As regards Swiss currency, see page 100.

LANGUAGE.—Italy is a country where many dialects are commonly spoken, even among the educated classes. Tuscan, however, is the recognised official speech everywhere, and though the tourist may chance to hear local names for various objects in different parts, the Tuscan form given in the following pages will be understood in all places.

WAR CEMETERIES.—Since the end of the last war another reason for visiting Italy has been added to the innumerable ones which already existed. Many British and Dominion travellers now go to Italy on pilgrimage, to visit one or other of those war cemeteries in which their loved ones have been finally laid to rest.

Forty-two of these cemeteries are scattered up and down the country, thirty-eight on the mainland, from Udine in the far north to Salerno and Bari in the south, one in Sardinia (just outside Cagliari) and three in Sicily. These cemeteries are under the care of the Imperial War Graves Commission and an invaluable pamphlet (" The War Graves of the British Commonwealth in Italy ") was published in Rome in 1948 by the CIT (Compagnia Italiana Turismo) and may be obtained from their offices. Most of these cemeteries lie near towns or large villages (e.g., the " Arrow Route Cemetery " lies beside the regular motor road from Florence to Fiesole) and are easily reached ; a few, however, are at some distance from towns and the following notes may prove helpful.

The *Arezzo* military cemetery is 9 kilometres west of Arezzo and lies in the fields about 40 metres south of the main Arezzo-Florence road.

About 25 kilometres from Arezzo lies the *Foiano della Chiana* cemetery, near the village of that name ; the route to follow from Arezzo is the main road to Siena as far as the village of Pieve del Toppo and then branch south to Foiano.

The *Coriano Ridge* cemetery is some 5 kilometres from Riccione (province of Forlì), but it is a cross-country journey from the town and the visitor should make inquiries in Riccione.

Also in the province of Forlì is the *Meldola* cemetery. The visitor coming by car should follow the main Bologna-Rimini road to the village of Ronco, near Forlì, and then take the secondary road to Meldola ; about 7 kilometres down this a lane branches to the left, just after a stream has been crossed ; the cemetery lies on the left side of the lane.

The *Bari* cemetery is about 8 kilometres south of Bari, on the road to Taranto. The visitor should leave this road and take a country lane on the right, leading to Carbonara di Bari.

The *Montecchio* cemetery, near Pesaro, is reached by following the main road from Pesaro to Rimini for 3 kilometres, then turning sharp left on to the secondary road leading to Urbino. Ten kilometres along this road the cemetery lies on the right-hand side.

The *Orvieto* cemetery, to the west of the old city, lies beyond the river Paglia. The visitor who follows the road to Todi should branch right beyond the river and follow a country lane till the cemetery is seen in a depression between low hills.

The *Ravenna* cemetery is reached by following the main road from Ravenna to Ferrara for 8 kilometres, when a lane branches left to the village of La Tagliata. The cemetery lies in the fields about 1½ kilometres down this lane, on the left. This same main Ravenna-Ferrara road leads to the *Villanova* Canadian cemetery. The visitor should turn sharp left after crossing the Lamone river near Mezzano. The cemetery lies just beyond Villanova village.

The *Salerno* cemetery is situated 15 kilometres east of Salerno, on the main road from this town to Battipaglia.

The *Sangro River* cemetery lies on a high ridge above the river, near the little coastal town of Torino di Sangro, on the main Adriatic coast railway, south of Ortona.

The *Santerno Valley* cemetery is reached from the Futa Pass main route from Florence to Bologna. The visitor coming from Florence should leave this road $5\frac{1}{2}$ kilometres beyond the pass and should proceed through Firenzuola down the Santerno river valley till the cemetery appears on the right, some 15 kilometres farther on.

TRAVELLING

THE FRONTIER

Which is the frontier station ?	Qual'è la stazione di frontiera ?
kwah'lay lah staht-see-oh'nay dee fron-tee-ay'rah ?	
When do we arrive at the frontier ?	Quando arriviamo alla frontiera ?
kwahn'doh ahr-ree-vee-ah'moh ahl'lah fron-tee-ay'rah ?	
Have we to leave the train ?	Dobbiamo scendere dal treno ?
dob-bee-ah'moh shen'day-ray dahl tray'noh ?	
Are passports examined on the train ?	I passaporti vengono controllati in treno ?
ee pass-sah-porr'tee veng'goh-noh kon-troll-lah'tee in tray'noh ?	
Here is my passport.	Ecco il mio passaporto.
eck'koh eel mee'oh pass-sah-porr'toh.	

CUSTOMS (LA DOGANA)

Have you anything to declare ?	Ha qualcosa da dichiarare ?
ah kwahl-koh'zah dah dee-kee-ah-rah'ray ?	
Shall I open everything ?	Devo aprire tutto ?
day'voh ah-pree'ray toot'toh ?	
Take down that case, please.	Tiri giù quella valigia, per favore.
tee'ree joo kwell'lah vah-lee-jah, pehr fah-vor'ray.	
I have nothing to declare.	Non ho nulla da dichiarare.
non oh nool'lah dah dee-kee-ah-rah'ray.	
Where are you going ?	Dove va Lei ? (*sing.*) ; vanno Loro ? (*plur.*).
doh'vay vah lay'ee (vahn'noh lor'roh) ?	
I am (we are) going straight through to —.	Vado (andiamo) direttamente a ——.
Vah'doh (ahn-dee-ah'moh) dee-ret-tah-men'tay ah . . .	

17

| I have this box of cigarettes, this tobacco. | Ho questa scatola di sigarette, questo tabacco. |

oh kwess'tah skah'toh-lah dee see-gah-ret'tay, kwess'toh tah-bahk'koh.

| You are not allowed to bring in more than one hundred cigarettes. | Non è permesso portare più di cento sigarette. |

non ay pehr-mess'soh porr-tah'ray pee-oo'dee chen'toh see-gah-ret'tay.

| What food have you? | Ha provviste? |

ah prov-vee'stay?

| I have two pounds of tea (of sugar) for my own use. | Ho due libbre di tè (di zucchero) per il mio uso personale. |

oh doo'ay leeb'bray dee tay (dee zook'kay-roh) pehr eel mee'oh oo'zoh pehr-soh-nah'lay.

| How much must I pay? | Quanto devo pagare? |

kwahn'toh day'voh pah-gah'ray?

| There are only personal effects. | Ci sono solo effetti personali. |

chee soh'noh soh'loh ef-fet'tee pehr-soh-nah'lee.

| They have all been used. | Sono tutti usati. |

soh'noh toot'tee oo-zah'tee.

ON THE TRAIN

| May I open (shut) the window? | Posso aprire (chiudere) la finestra? |

poss'soh ah-pree'ray (chee-oo'day-ray) lah fee-ness'trah?

| It is hot (cold). | Fa caldo (freddo). |

fah kahl'doh (fred'doh).

| There is a draught. | C'è corrente. |

chay kor-ren'tay.

| Please would you shut (open) the door? | Per favore, vuol chiudere (aprire) la porta? |

pehr fah-vor'ray, voo-ohl'kee-oo'day-ray (ah-pree'ray) lah porr'tah?

| Thank you. | Grazie. |

graht'see-ay.

Do you mind my smoking? | Permette che io fumi ?

pehr-met'tay kay ee'oh foo'mee ?

Excuse me, I can't bear tobacco smoke. | Mi scusi, non posso sopportare il fumo del tabacco.

mee skoo'zee, non poss'soh sop-porr-tah'ray eel foo'moh dell tah-bahk'koh.

Please would you turn the light off (on) ? | Per favore, vuole spegnere (accendere) la luce?

pehr fah-vor'ray, voo-ohl'spayn'yay-ray (ahch-chen'day-ray) lah loo'chay ?

Where are we now ? | Dove siamo ora ?

doh'vay see-ah'moh or'rah ?

Are we late (on time) ? | Siamo in ritardo (in orario) ?

see-ah'moh in ree-tahr'doh (in or-rah'ree-oh) ?

When do we arrive at —? | Quando arriveremo a —?

kwahn'doh ahr-ree-vay-ray'-moh ah . . . ?

How long does the train stop ? | Quanto tempo si ferma il treno ?

kwahn'toh tem'poh see fehr'mah eel tray'noh ?

Have I time to go to the buffet ? (to the telegraph office ?) | Ho tempo di andare al ristorante ? (all' ufficio telegrafico ?)

oh tem'poh dee ahn-dah'ray ahl ree-stoh-rahn'tay ? (ahl-loo-fee'choh tay-lay-grah'fee-koh ?)

Which way is the lavatory, please ? | Per favore, da che parte è la ritirata ?

pehr fah-vor'ray, dah kay pahr'tay ay lah ree-tee-rah'tah ?

Is this seat free ? | È libero questo posto ?

ay lee'bay-roh kwess'toh poss'toh ?

This seat is taken. | Questo posto è occupato.

kwess'toh poss'toh ay ock-koo-pah'toh.

The ticket collector (guard). | Il controllore.

eel kon-troll-lor'ray.

The inspector (head guard). | Il capotreno.

eel kah-poh-tray'noh.

The stationmaster.	Il capo-stazione.

eel kah-poh-staht-see-oh'nay.

Car, compartment.	Vettura, scompartimento.

vet-too'rah. skom-pahr-tee-men'toh.

A pillow.	Un cuscino.

oon koo-shee'noh.

A seat.	Un posto.

oon poss'toh.

A berth.	Una cuccetta.

oo'nah kooch-chet'tah.

Through carriage.	Carrozza diretta.

kahr-rot'sah dee-ret'tah.

DIFFICULTIES

I cannot find my ticket.	Non riesco a trovare il mio biglietto.

non ree-ess'koh ah troh-vah'ray eel mee'oh beel-yet'toh.

I showed it to the guard after we had left ——.	L'ho mostrato al controllore dopo ——.

loh moss-trah'toh ahl kon-troll-loh'ray doh'poh . . .

I got in at ——.	Sono salito a ——.

soh'noh sah-lee'toh ah . . .

I am travelling to ——.	Vado a ——.

vah'doh ah . . .

I missed the connection for ——.	Ho perduto la coincidenza per ——.

oh pehr-doo'toh lah koh-een-chee-dent'sah pehr .

What time will the next train leave ?	A che ora c'è un altro treno ?

ah kay or'rah chay oon ahl'troh tray'noh ?

I left a suitcase (an overcoat, an umbrella, a camera) in the train from ——.	Ho dimenticato una valigia (un soprabito, un ombrello, una macchina fotografica) sul treno da ——.

oh dee-men-tee-kah'toh oo'nah vah-lee'jah (oon soh-prah'bee-toh, oon om-brell'loh, oo'nah mahk'kee-nah foh-toh-grah'fee-kah) sool tray'noh dah . . .

Where is the lost property office ? | Dov'e ... etti
ritrova...

doh-vay'loof-fee'choh od-jet'tee ree-troh-... e ?

THE DINING CAR

Where is the dining car ? | Dov'è il vaggone risto-
rante ?

doh-vay'eel vah-goh'nay ree-stoh-rahn'tay ?

What time is the first (second) service ? | A che ora è la prima (seconda) serie ?

ah kay or'rah ay lah pree'mah (say-kon'dah) say'ree-ay ?

Give me a ticket for the first (second) service. | Mi dia un posto per il primo (secondo) servizio.

mee dee'ah oon poss'toh pehr eel pree'moh (say-kon'doh) sehr-veet'see-oh.

I have no Italian money ; can I pay in French (Swiss) francs ? | Non no danaro italiano ; posso pagare in franchi francesi (svizzeri) ?

non oh dah-nah'roh ee-tah-lee-ah'noh ; poss'soh pah-gah'ray in frahng'kee frahn-chay'zee (sveet'say-ree) ?

Can you change a travel-ler's cheque ? | Può cambiare un . . . ?

poo-oh' kahm-bee-ah'ray oon (*as in English*) ?

AT THE STATION

Have we arrived at ——? | Siamo arrivati a —— ?

see-ah'moh ahr-ree-vah'tee ah . . . ?

Porter ! | Facchino !

fahk'kee-noh !

Take this luggage. | Prenda questi bagagli.

pren'dah kwess'tee bah-gahl'yee.

There are —— (*for num-bers, see p.* 98) cases. | Ci sono —— colli.

chee soh'noh —— koll'lee.

Don't take that one. | Non prenda quello.

non pren'dah kwell'loh.

	Io prendo questo.
	pren'doh kwess'toh.
Handle	Stia attento.
	stee'ah aht-ten'toh.
Show me the way to the cloakroom.	Mi conduca al deposito.
mee kon-doo'kah ahl day-poh' zee-toh.	
Take them to the cloakroom.	Li porti al deposito.
lee porr'tee ahl day-poh'zee-toh.	
I want to leave this in the cloakroom.	Vorrei lasciare questo al deposito.
vor-ray'ee lah-shah'ray kwess'toh ahl day-poh'zee-toh.	

AT THE CLOAKROOM

I want to leave these cases here.	Vorrei lasciare qui questi colli.
vor-ray'ee lah-shah'ray kwee kwess'tee koll'lee.	
Not this one.	Questo no.[1]
kwess'toh no.	
Must I pay now ?	Devo pagare ora ?
day'voh pah-gah'ray or'rah ?	
I want to take out my luggage.	Desidero ritirare il mio bagaglio.
day-zee'day-roh ree-tee-rah'ray eel mee'oh bah-gahl'yoh.	
That one. Yes.	Quello. Si.
kwell'loh. see.	
I am in a hurry.	Ho fretta.
oh fret'tah.	
My train leaves in a few minutes.	Il mio treno parte fra pochi minuti.
eel mee'oh tray'noh pahr'tay frah poh'kee mee-noo'tee.	
How much is that ?	Quanto fa ?
kwahn'toh fah ?	
Take this to the train for—.	Porti questo al treno per—.
porr'tee kwess'toh ahl tray'noh pehr . . .	

[1] The Italian negative monosyllable *no* has a very open sound, like the English *no-* in *nor.*

REGISTERED LUGGAGE

I have some luggage in the van. | Ho dei bagagli nel bagagliaio.

oh day'ee, bah-gahl'yee nell bah-gahl-yah'yoh.

Come with me to get it out. | Venga con me a ritirarli.

veng'gah kon may ah ree-tee-rahr'lee.

Here is my luggage ticket. | Ecco il mio scontrino.

eck'koh eel mee'oh skon-tree'noh.

Where is the luggage office? | Dov'è l'ufficio bagagli ?

doh-vay'loof-fee'choh bah-gahl'yee ?

I want to register this trunk for ——. | Desidero assicurare questo baule per ——.

day-zee'day-roh ahs-see-koo-rah'ray kwess'toh bah-oo'lay pehr . . .

I have two tickets. | Ho due biglietti.

oh doo'ay beel-yet'tee.

I am leaving by the —— o'clock train. | Parto con il treno delle ——.

pahr'toh kon eel tray'noh dell'lay . . .

How much have I to pay. | Quanto devo pagare ?

kwahn'toh day'voh pah-gah'ray ?

LEAVING BY TRAIN

Could you tell me the way to the station for — ? | Potrebbe indicarmi dov'è la stazione per —— ?

poh-treb'bay in-dee-kahr'mee doh-vay' lah staht-see-oh'nay pehr . . . ?

Is this the station for —— ? | E' questa la stazione per —— ?

ay kwess'tah lah staht-see-oh'nay pehr . . . ?

Take my luggage. | Prenda il mio bagaglio.

pren'dah eel mee'oh bah-gahl'yoh.

Wait here. | Aspetti qui.

ah-spet'tee kwee.

Where is the departure time-table ? | Dov'è l'orario delle partenze ?

doh-vay' lor-rah'ree-oh dell'lay pahr-tent'say ?

Where is the booking office ?	Dov'è la biglietteria ?

doh-vay' lah beel-yet-tay-ree'ah ?

At what platform is the train for —— ?	Su quale binario è il treno per —— ?

soo kwah'lay bee-nah'ree-oh ay eel tray'noh pehr . . . ?

Is this the train for—— ?	E' questo il treno per —— ?

ay kwess'toh eel tray'noh pehr . . . ?

What time does the train for —— leave ?	A che ora parte il treno per —— ?

ah kay or'rah pahr'tay eel tray'noh pehr . . . ?

What time is the train from —— due ?	A che ora arriva il treno da —— ?

ah kay or'rah ahr-ree'vah eel tray'noh dah . . . ?

Is the train from —— up to time ?	È in orario il treno da —— ?

ay in or-rah'ree-oh eel tray'noh dah . . . ?

AT THE BOOKING OFFICE

I want a first (second, third) class single (return) ticket to ——.	Desidero un biglietto di prima (seconda, terza) classe andata (andata e ritorno) per ——.

day-zee'day-roh oon beel-yet'toh dee pree'mah (say-kon'dah, tehrt'sah) klahs'say ahn-dah'tah (ahn-dah'tah ay ree-torr'noh) pehr . . .

I wish to travel by the —— o'clock train.	Intendo partire con il treno delle ——.

in-ten'doh pahr-tee'ray kon eel tray'noh dell'lay . . .

I am leaving to-night (to-morrow).	Parto stasera (domani).

pahr'toh stah-say'rah (doh-mah'nee).

Shall I have to change ? Where ?	Devo cambiar treno ? Dove ?

day'voh kahm-bee-ahr'tray'noh ? doh'vay ?

Is there a connection at once ?	C'è subito la coincidenza ?

chay soo'bee-toh lah koh-in-chee-dent' sah ?

Can I travel by express trains with this ticket ?	È valido anche per i direttissimi questo biglietto ?

ay vah'lee-doh ahng'kay pehr ee dee-ret-tees'see-mee kwess'toh beel-yet'toh ?

How long is it available ?	Per quanto tempo è valido ?

pehr kwahn'toh tem'poh ay vah'lee-doh ?

Am I entitled to break my journey ?	Ho diritto a fermate intermedie ?

oh dee-reet'toh ah fehr-mah'tay in-tehr-may'dee-ay ?

Have I to pay a supplement on this train ?	Devo pagare il supplemento su questo treno ?

day'voh pah-gah'ray eel soop-play-men'toh soo kwess'toh tray'noh ?

SEATS

Can seats be reserved on the train for —— ?	Si possono prenotare posti sul treno per — ?

see poss'soh-noh pray-noh-tah'ray poss'tee sool tray'noh pehr . . . ?

I want to reserve a place.	Desidero prenotare un posto.

day-zee'day-roh pray-noh-tah'ray oon poss'toh.

I have two seats reserved.	Ho prenotato due posti.

oh pray-noh-tah'toh doo'ay poss'tee.

These are the numbers.	Questi sono i numeri.

kwess'tee soh'noh ee noo'may-ree.

Find me two seats, first (second, third) class.	Mi trovi due posti di prima (seconda, terza) classe.

mee troh'vee doo'ay poss'tee dee pree'mah (say-kon'dah, tehrt'sah) klahs'say.

Smoker. Non-smoker.	Fumatori. Vietato fumare.

foo-mah-tor'ree. vee-ay-tah'toh foo-mah'ray.

A corner seat.	Un posto d'angolo.

oon poss'toh dahng'goh-loh.

Facing the engine. (Back to the engine.)	In direzione di marcia. (All'indietro.)

in dee-ret-see-oh'nay dee mahr'chah (ahl-lin-dee-ay'troh).

Not near the engine.	Non vicino alla loco-motiva.

non vee-chee'noh ahl'lah loh-koh-moh-tee'vah.

Put this on the rack.	Metta questo sulla rete.

met'tah kwess'toh sool'lah ray'tay.

SLEEPERS

Is there a sleeping car on the train ?	Il treno ha vagoni letto ?

eel tray'noh ah vah-goh'nee let'toh ?

Are there second-class sleepers ?	Vi sono posti di seconda classe ?

vee soh'noh poss'tee dee say-kon'dah klahs'say ?

What is the supplement as far as —— ?	Che supplemento pago fino a —— ?

kay soop-play-men'toh pah'goh fee'noh ah . . . ?

I want to reserve a berth.	Desidero prenotare un posto.

day-zee'day-roh pray-noh-tah'ray oon poss'toh.

A sleeping compartment.	Una cabina.

oo'nah kah-bee'nah.

The upper (lower) berth.	La cuccetta superiore (inferiore).

lah kooch-chet'tah soo-pay-ree-or'ray (in-fay-ree-or'ray).

TRAVELLING BY BOAT

Is there a boat service between —— and —?	C'è servizio di battello tra —— e ——?

Chay sehr-veet'see-oh dee baht-tell'loh trah —— ay ——?

When does the boat leave ?	Quando parte il battello ?

kwahn'doh pahr'tay eel baht-tell'loh ?

When does it arrive at —?	Quando arriva a ——?

kwahn'doh ahr-ree'vah ah . . . ?

Can I land at ——?	Posso scendere a ——?

poss'soh shen'day-ray ah . . . ?

Can I have meals on board ?	C'è servizio di ristorante ?

chay sehr-veet'see-oh dee ree-stor-rahn'tay ?

Where is the landing stage?	Dov'è l'imbarcatoio ?

doh-vay' lim-bahr-kah-toy'yoh ?

Can I have a deck-chair ?	Posso avere una sedia a sdraio ?

poss'soh ah-vay'ray oo'nah say'dee-ah ah zdrah'yoh ?

AIR TRAVEL

Where is the air company's office ?	Dove sono gli uffici dell'aviolinea ?

doh'vay soh'noh lyee oof-fee'chee dell-lah-vee-oh-lee'nay-ah ?

Is there a motor coach service to the aerodrome ?	Vi è servizio di autobus per l'aeroporto ?

vee ay sehr-veet'see-oh dow'toh-booss pehr lah-ay-roh-porr'toh ?

Aeroplane. Seaplane. Pilot.	Aeroplano. [Apparecchio.] Idrovolante. Pilota.

ah-ay-roh-plah'noh (ahp-pah-reck'kee-oh). ee-droh-voh-lahn'tay. pee-loh'tah.

Is there a daily service to ——?	Vi è servizio giornaliero per ——?

vee ay sehr-veet'see-oh jorr-nah-lee-ay'roh pehr . . . ?

When does it start ?	Quando parte ?

kwahn'doh pahr'tay ?

When do we arrive at —?	Quando si arriva a ——?

kwahn'doh see ahr-ree'vah ah . . . ?

Can we get anything to eat on board ?	Si può avere qualcosa da mangiare a bordo ?

see poo-oh' ah-vay'ray kwahl-koh' zah dah mahn-jah'ray ah borr'doh ?

What is the maximum allowance of luggage ?	Qual'è il massimo di bagaglio consentito ?

kwah-lay'eel mahs'see-moh dee bah-gahl'yoh kon-sen-tee'toh ?

I feel sick.	Mi sento male.

mee sen'toh mah'lay.

Have you a paper bag for air-sickness ?	Ha un sacchetto ?

ah oon sahk-ket'toh ?

One of these bags is placed in front of each seat. In view of the noise of the engines, cotton wool is usually available for the ears.

ACCOMMODATION

A complete list of Italian hotels, with categories, charges, etc. is published by E.N.I.T. (Ente Nazionale dell'Industria del Turismo), and in large towns this association usually has offices where much useful information may be obtained.

For students and young people visiting Italy a number of " Youth Hostels " (Alberghi della Gioventù, ahl-behr ghee dell'lah joh-ven-too') have now been set up and are open to all members of Youth Organisations.

About 50 have already been opened ; below are the names of a few of them:

Bardonecchia : P.A. Azienda Soggiorno.

La Thuile : P.A. Errani Paris.

Verrand (Val d'Aosta) : P.A. Ulisse Brunod.

Gardone Riviera (Lake Garda) : P.A. Collegio Tuminelli (for men only).

Cavi di Lavagna (near Genoa) : M.A. Gabriella Belloni, via Aurelia 161.

Porto Venere (Gulf of Spezzia) : P.A. Comitato A.I.G., presso E.P.T., La Spezia.

Lerici (Gulf of Spezzia) : P.A. Comitato A.I.G., presso
E.P.T., La Spezzia.
Florence : Palazzo Cristallo, Piazza Beccaria.
Rome : Via Ostiense, 263/c.
Naples : Albergo Grilli, via Galileo Ferraris.

The charge per night is now 180 *(heating in winter* 25) *lire;
sheets* 50 *lire. There is often use of kitchen, and in each town
there are special restaurants where meals may be obtained very
cheaply. Information may be had at the hostels.*

FROM STATION TO HOTEL

Porter, take this luggage and call me a taxi. | Facchino, prenda questi bagagli e mi chiami un tassì (una vettura).

fahk-kee'noh, pren'dah kwess'tee bah-gahl'yee ay mee kee-ah'mee oon tahs-see' (oo'nah vet-too'rah).

Can you carry this luggage to the — Hotel ? | Mi può portare questi bagagli fino all'albergo — ?

mee poo-oh' porr-tah'ray kwess'tee bah-gahl'yee fee'noh ahl lahl-behr'goh ——?

To the —— Hotel. | All'albergo ——.

ahl lahl-behr'goh ——.

Which is the best hotel ? | Qual'è l'albergo migliore?

kwah-lay' lahl-behr'goh meel-yor'ray ?

I want a good hotel, not too dear. | Vorrei un buon albergo, non troppo caro.

vor-ray'ee oon boo-ohn' ahl-behr'goh, non trop'poh kah'roh.

I want to be in the centre of the town. | Vorrei stare nel centro della città.

vor-ray'ee stah'ray nell chen'troh dell'lah chit-tah'.

I don't want to be in a noisy part. | Non voglio stare in un quartiere rumoroso.

non voll'yoh stah'ray in oon kwahr-tee-ay'ray roo-moh-roh'zoh.

ENGAGING ROOMS

Where is the office ? | Dov'è la direzione ?

doh-vay' lah dee-ret-see-oh'nay ?

| I want a room with a single bed (with a double bed). | Desidero una camera a un letto (con letto matrimoniale). |

day-zee'day-roh oo'nah kah'may-rah ah oon let'toh (kon let'toh mah-tree-moh-nee-ah'lay).

| A room with two beds. | Una camera a due letti. |

oo'nah kah'may-rah ah doo'ay let'tee.

| Two single-bedded rooms. | Due camere a un letto. |

doo'ay kah'may-ray ah oon let'toh.

| With own bath.   With sitting-room. | Con bagno particolare. Con salottino. |

kon bahn'yoh pahr-tee-koh-lah'ray. kon sah-lot-tee'noh.

| Is bath accommodation near ? | È vicina la stanza da bagno ? |

ay vee-chee'nah lah stahnt'sah dah bahn' yoh ?

| What is the price of this room ? | Quanto costa questa camera ? |

kwahn'toh koss'tah kwess'tah kah'may-rah ?

| Have you anything cheaper (better) ? | Non ne ha un'altra meno cara (migliore) ? |

non nay ah oo-nahl'trah may'noh kah'rah (meel-yor'ray) ?

| On what floor ? | A che piano ? |

ah kay pee-ah'noh ?

| Is there a lift ? | C'è l'ascensore ? |

chay lah-shen-sor'ray ?

| Is there central heating ? | C'è riscaldamento |

chay ree-skahl-dah-men'toh ?

| Is there running water in the rooms ? | C'è acqua corrente nelle camere ? |

chay ahk'kwah kor-ren'tay nell'lay kah'may-ray ?

| Let me see the room. | Mi faccia vedere la camera. |

mee fahch'chah vay-day'ray lah kah'may-rah.

| This room is too small (dark). | Questa camera è troppo piccola (buia). |

kwess'tah kah'may-rah ay trop'poh peek'koh-lah (boo'yah).

I do not like this room.	Questa camera non mi piace.

kwess'tah kah'may-rah non mee pee-ah'chay.

Have you a room facing the garden (the court-yard, the street)?	Ha una camera che dà sul giardino (sul cor-tile, sulla strada)?

ah oo'nah kah'may-rah kay dah sool jahr-dee'noh (sool korr-tee'lay, sool'lah strah'dah)?

I want a room lower down (higher up).	Vorrei una camera al piano inferiore (superiore).

Vor-ray'ee oo'nah kah'may-rah ahl pee-ah'noh in-fay-ree-or'ray (soo-pay-ree-or'ray).

On the first (second, third, fourth) floor.	Al primo (secondo, terzo, quarto) piano.

ahl pree'moh (say-kon'doh, tehrt'soh, kwahr'toh) pee-ah'noh.

I will take this.	Prendo questa.

pren'doh kwess'tah.

For to-night only.	Per stanotte soltanto.

pehr stah-not'tay soll-tahn'toh.

I will stay a few days.	Mi fermerò qualche giorno.

mee fehr-may-roh' kwahl'kay jorr'noh.

How much do you charge per day, includ-ing meals?	Quanto chiede al giorno per la pensione com-pleta?

kwahn'toh kee-ay'day ahl jorr'noh pehr lah pen-see-oh'nay kom-play'tah?

What are your terms for a longer stay?	Quanto fa pagare per un soggiorno prolungato?

kwahn'toh fah pah-gah'ray pehr oon sod-jorr'noh proh-loong-gah'toh?

Is attendance included?	E' compreso il servizio?

ay kom-pray'zoh eel sehr-veet'see-oh?

Is there a tourists' tax to be paid?	Si paga la tassa di sog-giorno?

see pah'gah lah tahs'sah dee sod-jorr'noh?

| I have some heavy luggage at the station. | Ho dei bagagli alla stazione. |

oh day'ee bah-gahl'yee ahl'lah staht-see-oh'nay.

| Here is the ticket. | Ecco lo scontrino. |

eck'koh loh skon-tree'noh.

| Have my luggage taken up. | Mi faccia portar su il bagaglio. |

mee fahch'chah porr-tahr' soo eel bah-gahl'yoh.

| What is the number of my room? | Che numero ha la mia camera? |

kay noo'may-roh ah lah mee'ah kah may-rah?

THE CHAMBERMAID

| Are you the chambermaid? | E' Lei la cameriera? |

ay lay'ee lah kah-may-ree-ay'rah?

| Bring me a pillow. | Mi porti un guanciale. |

mee porr'tee oon gwahn-chah'lay.

| Another blanket, sheets. | Un'altra coperta, delle lenzuola. |

oo-nahl'trah koh-pehr'tah, dell'lay lent-soo-oh'lah.

| Some hot water, soap, towels. | Dell'acqua calda, del sapone, degli asciugamani. |

dell-lahk'kwah kahl'dah, dell sah-poh'nay, dayl'yee ah-shoo-gah-mah'nee.

| I want to have a bath. | Vorrei fare il bagno. |

vor-ray'ee fah'ray eel bahn'yoh.

| I want to be called to-morrow at —— o'clock. | Desidero essere svegliato domani alle ——. |

day-zee'day-roh ess'say-ray svayl-yah'toh doh-mah'nee ahl'lay . . .

LAUNDRY

For washing list, see under " Clothing," page 74—*and " General Shopping Vocabulary," page* 80.

I have some things to be washed ; here is the list.	Ho della biancheria da far lavare ; ecco la nota.

oh dell'lah bee-ahng-kay-ree'ah dah fahr lah-vah'ray ; eck'koh lah noh'tah.

When shall I have them back ?	Quando l'avrò di ritorno ?

kwahn'doh lah-vroh'dee ree-torr'noh ?

I am leaving on (*days of the week, see p.* 103).	Parto ——.

pahr'toh . . .

MENDING AND CLEANING

This needs mending.	Questo ha bisogno di essere rammendato.

kwess'toh ah bee-zohn'yoh dee ess'say-ray rahm-men-dah'toh.

Can you have it mended in the hotel for me ?	Può farmelo rammendare in albergo ?

poo-oh' fahr'may-loh rahm-men-dah'ray in ahl-behr'goh ?

I have a button off.	Mi si è staccato un bottone.

mee see ay stahk-kah'toh oon bot-toh'nay.

Can you sew it on ?	Può attaccarlo ?

poo-oh' aht-tahk-kahr' loh ?

Will you have my clothes brushed (pressed) ?	Mi fa spazzolare (stirare) il mio vestito ?

mee fah spaht-soh-lah'ray (stee-rah'ray) eel mee'oh vess-tee'toh ?

I will leave them out.	Lo lascerò fuori.

loh lah-shay-roh' foo-or'ree.

Have my boots (shoes) cleaned.	Mi faccia lustrare le scarpe.

mee fahch'chah loo-strah'ray lay skahr'pay.

THE OFFICE

My name is ——.	Mi chiamo ——.

mee kee-ah'moh . . .

Will you fill in the registration card for me ?	Vuole riempire Lei la scheda per me ?

voo-oh'lay ree-em-pee'ray lay'ee lah skay'dah pehr may ?

Here is my passport.	Ecco il mio passaporto.

eck'koh eel mee'oh pass-sah-porr'toh.

Will you attend to my registration at the police station ?	Vuole provvedere alla mia dichiarazione di soggiorno in Questura ?

voo-oh'lay prov-vay-day'ray ahl'lah mee'ah dee-kee-ah-raht-see-oh'nay dee sod-jorr'noh in kwess-too'rah ?

I have room No. ——.	Ho la camera numero —.

oh lah kah'may-rah noo'may-roh ——.

Are there any letters for me ?	Ci sono lettere per me ?

chee soh'noh let'tay-ray pehr may ?

Will you give me the key of my room ?	Mi vuol dare la chiave della mia camera ?

mee voo-ohl' dah'ray lah kee-ah'vay dell'lah mee'ah kah'may rah ?

THE HALL PORTER

I want to have these letters posted.	Vorrei far impostare queste lettere.

Vor-ray'ee fahr im-poss-tah'ray kwess'tay let'tay-ray.

Will you put the stamps on ?	Vuole mettere i francobolli ?

voo-oh'lay met'tay-ray ee frahng-koh-boll'lee ?

How much is that ?	Quanto fa ?

kwahn'toh fah ?

I want to send a telegram.	Vorrei spedire un telegramma.

Vor-ray'ee spay-dee'ray oon tay-lay-grahm'mah.

Has any one called to see me ?	C'è stato qualcuno a cercarmi ?

chay stah'toh kwahl-koo'noh ah chehr-kahr'mee ?

I shall be back in an hour's time.	Sarò di ritorno fra un'ora.

sah-roh' dee ree-torr'noh frah oo-nor'rah.

If any one calls for me, please ask them to wait.	Se qualcuno chiede di me, lo preghi di aspettarmi.

say kwahl-koo'noh kee-ay'day dee may, loh pray'ghee dee ah-spet-tahr'mee.

Get me a taxi, please.	Mi chiami un tassì, per favore.

mee kee-ah'mee oon tahs-see', pehr fah-vor'ray.

A cab.	Una vettura.

oo'nah vet-too'rah.

Which is the shortest way to get to ——?	Qual'è la via più breve per andare a ——?

kwah-lay' lah vee'ah pee-oo' bray'vay pehr ahn-dah'ray ah . . . ?

Have you a map of the town?	Ha una pianta della città?

ah oo'nah pee-ahn'tah dell'lah chit-tah'?

Have you a telephone directory?	Ha un elenco telefonico?

ah oon ay-leng'koh tay-lay-foh' nee-koh?

LEAVING THE HOTEL

I have to leave to-morrow early.	Devo partire domani mattina di buon'ora.

day'voh pahr-tee'ray doh-mah'nee maht-tee'nah dee boo-oh-nor'rah.

Please have my bill made out.	Mi faccia preparare il conto.

mee fahch'chah pray-pah-rah'ray eel kon'toh.

I am taking the —— o'clock train for ——.	Prendo il treno delle —— per ——.

pren'doh eel tray'noh dell'lay —— pehr ——.

Will you get the ticket for me?	Potrebbe mandare qualcuno a farmi il biglietto?

poh-treb'bay mahn-dah'ray kwahl-koo'noh ah fahr'mee eel beel-yet'toh?

| Will you have my luggage registered ? | Mi fa assicurare il mio bagaglio ? |

mee fah ahs-see-koo-rah'ray eel mee'oh bah-gahl'yoh.

| I shall need a taxi to take me to the station. | Avrò bisogna di un tassì per andare alla stazione. |

ah-vroh' bee-zohn'yoh dee oon tahs-see' pehr ahn-dah'ray ahl'lah staht-see-oh'nay.

| How much does my bill come to ? | Quanto è il mio conto ? |

kwahn'toh ay eel mee'oh kon'toh ?

| Will you take English money (a traveller's cheque) ? | Prende valuta inglese (un traveller's cheque) ? |

pren'day vah-loo'tah eeng-glay'zay (oon traveller's cheque) ?

| Is there a charge for service ? | È compreso il servizio ? |

ay kom-pray'zoh eel sehr-veet'see-oh ?

| Give me some small change. | Mi dia degli spiccioli. |

mee dee'ah dayl'yee speech'choh-lee.

| Keep this for yourself. | Tenga questo per sè. |

teng'gah kwess'toh pehr say.

| Have my luggage brought down. | Faccia portar giù le mie valige. |

fahch'chah porr-tahr' joo lay mee'ay vah-lee'jay.

| Send my luggage to the station, please. | Mi mandi il bagaglio alla stazione, per favore. |

mee mahn'dee eel bah-gahl' yoh ahl'lah staht-see-oh'nay, pehr fah-vor'ray.

| Please have any letters sent on to this address. | Mi faccia proseguire tutta la corrisponden- za a questo indirizzo. |

mee fahch'chah proh-say-gwee'ray toot'tah la kor-ree-spon- dent'sah ah kwess'toh een-dee-reet'soh.

| Thank you and good-bye. | Grazie e arrivederla. |

graht'see-ay ay ahr-ree-vay-dehr'lah.

DIFFICULTIES

What are these charges for?	Questo per che cosa è ?

kwess'toh pehr kay koh'zah ay ?

I think you have made a mistake.	Mi pare che ci sia un errore.

mee pah'ray kay chee see'ah oon ehr-ror'ray.

I did not have ——.	Io non ho avuto ——.

ee'oh non oh ah-voo'toh . . .

You said the room cost only ——.	Mi aveva detto che la camera era —— lire soltanto.

mee ah-vay'vah det'toh kay lah kah'may-rah eh'rah —— lee'ray soll-tahn'toh.

INLAND TRAVELLING— EXCURSIONS

INQUIRING THE WAY

Excuse me, which way do I go to ——?	Scusi, da che parte si va a ——?

skoo'zee, dah kay pahr'tay see vah ah . . . ?

Is this the right road to ——?	E' questa la strada per andare a ——?

ay kwess'tah lah strah'dah pehr ahn-dah'ray ah . . . ?

What street is this ?	Che via è questa ?

kay vee'ah ay kwess'tah ?

How far is it from here to ——?	Quanto c'è da qui a ——?

kwahn'toh chay dah kwee ah . . . ?

Can I walk or must I take the tram ?	Si può andare a piedi o bisogna prendere il tram ?

see poo-oh' ahn-dah'ray ah pee-ay'dee, oh bee-zohn'yah pren'day-ray eel trahm ?

Is —— far from here ?	—— è lontano da qui ?

—— ay lon-tah'noh dah kwee ?

Should I turn to the left (right)?	Devo voltare a sinistra (destra)?

day'voh voll-tah'ray ah see-nee'strah (dess'trah)?

Must I go straight on?	Devo andare diritto?

day'voh ahn-dah'ray dee-reet'toh?

DIFFICULTIES

I am lost.	Non trovo più la strada.

non troh'voh pee-oo' lah strah'dah.

I was going to ——.	Volevo andare a ——.

voh-lay'voh ahn-dah'ray ah ——.

I want to go back to —— (to the —— Hotel).	Desidero tornare a —— (all'Albergo ——).

day-zee'day-roh torr-nah'ray ah —— (ahl-lahl-behr'goh ——).

TRAVELLING BY TRAIN: *see " Leaving by Train," page 23, and " On the Train," page 18.*

CHARABANCS

Have you a list of the excursions?	Ha un programma delle gite?

ah oon proh-grahm'mah dell'lay jee'tay?

Is there a charabanc service to ——?	C'è servizio di autopull-man per ——?

chay sehr-veet'see-oh dee ow-toh-pool'mahn pehr ——?

What time does it start?	A che ora parte?

ah kay or'rah pahr'tay?

Where does one lunch?	Dove si fa colazione?

doh'vay see fah koh-laht-see-oh'nay?

I want to reserve a seat (two seats) for ——.	Desidero prenotare un posto (due posti) per ——.

day-zee'day-roh pray-noh-tah'ray oon poss'toh (doo'ay poss'tee) pehr ——.

What time shall we be back?	A che ora saremo di ritorno?

ah kay or'rah sah-ray'moh dee ree-torr'noh?

| Do you go if the weather is bad ? | Si parte anche col mal tempo ? |

see pahr'tay ahng'kay koll mahl tem'poh ?

BUS AND TRAM

| Where can I find a tram (bus) for —— ? | Dove posso prendere il tram (l'autobus) per —— ? |

doh'vay poss'soh pren'day-ray eel trahm (low'toh-booss) pehr . . . ?

| Where is the nearest (tram) stop ? | Dov'è la fermata (tran-viaria) più vicina ? |

doh-vay'lah fehr-mah'tah (trahn-vee-ah'ree-ah) pee-oo' vee-chee'nah ?

| Does this tram go to —— ? | Questo tram va a —— ? |

kwess'toh trham vah ah . . . ?

| I want to get off at ——. | Vorrei scendere a ——. |

vor-ray'ee shen'day-ray ah . . .

| I should like to take a drive through the main streets. | Vorrei fare un giro per le vie principali. |

vor-ray'ee fah'ray oon jee'roh pehr lay vee'ay preen-chee-pah'lee.

| Do you pass —— ? | Passa per —— ? |

pahs'sah pehr . . . ?

| Do you go near to —— ? | Passa vicino a —— ? |

pahs'sah vee-chee'noh ah . . . ?

TAXIS AND CABS
See also " Driving," page 48.

| Taxi ! Cab ! | Tassì ! Vettura ! |

tahs-see' ! vet-too'rah !

| Drive me to ——. | Mi conduca a ——. |

mee kon-doo'kah ah . . .

| Stop here. | Si fermi qui. |

see fehr'mee kwee.

| Wait here. | Aspetti qui. |

ah-spet'tee kwee.

| How much is that ? | Quanto fa ? |
| | kwahn'toh fah ? |

| Driver. Cabman. | Autista. Vetturino. |
| | ow-tee'stah. vet-too-ree'noh. |

DIFFICULTIES

| You ask too much. | Lei chiede troppo. |
| | lay'ee kee-ay'day trop'poh. |

| The taximeter registers less. | Il tassametro segna meno. |
| | eel tahs-sah'may-troh sayn'yah may'noh. |

| I don't understand this. | Non capisco questo. |
| | non kah-pee'skoh kwess'toh. |

| You are wrong. | Lei si sbaglia. |
| | lay'ee see sbahl'yah. |

| I will give you —— (*numbers, p.* 98) lire. | Le darò —— lire. |
| | lay dah-roh' —— lee'ray. |

| I shall call a policeman. | Ora chiamo un vigile. |
| | or'rah kee-ah'moh oon vee'jee-lay |

WALKING AND MOUNTAIN CLIMBING

There is ample scope in Italy for all lovers of natural beauties, ramblers, " hikers," and mountain climbers. The best seasons for walking are from April to June, and from September to early November, but mountain climbing on the Alps is best practised in summer months. A guide to the Italian mountains is published by the Club Alpino Italiano. This association has built on the Alps a number of refuge huts (rifugi, ree-foo'jee) and mountain inns.

The State Railways issue special week-end tickets (biglietti festivi, beel-yet tee fess-tee'vee), available from Friday midnight to Monday noon, to any point within a radius of 250 kilometres from most important towns at a reduction of 30 per cent. For information, apply to any railway station or tourist agency.

Can you tell me a good walk round here ? | Mi può indicare una bella passeggiata nei dintorni ?

mee poo-oh' in-dee-kah'ray oo'nah bell'lah pahs-sed-jah'tah nay'ee din-torr'nee ?

An easy walk. | Una passeggiata non troppo faticosa.

oo'nah pahs-sed-jah'tah non trop'poh fah-tee-koh'zah.

How long does the excursion take ? | Quanto tempo richiede l'escursione ?

kwahn'toh tem'poh ree-kee-ay'day less-koor-see-oh'nay ?

Is there a good view ? | Vi si gode una bella vista ?

vee see goh'day oo'nah bell'lah vee'stah ?

Where can I get something to eat ? | Dove posso trovare da mangiare ?

doh'vay poss'soh troh-vah'ray dah mahn-jah'ray ?

Cart track. | Strada carreggiabile.

strah'dah kahr-red-jah'bee-lay.

Mule track (bridle-path). | Mulattiera.

moo-laht-tee-ay'rah.

Foot-path. | Sentiero.

sen-tee-ay'roh.

A difficult climb. | Un'ascensione difficile.

oo-nah-shen-see-oh'nay deef-fee'chee-lay.

Do I need a guide ? | E'indispensabile prendere una guida ?

ay in-dee-spen-sah'bee-lay pren'day-ray oo'nah gwee'dah ?

Can you get me one for to-morrow ? | Può procurarmene una per domani ?

poo-oh' proh-koo-rahr' may-nay oo'nah pehr doh-mah'nee ?

Rucksack, alpenstock. | Sacco da montagna, bastone alpino.

sahk'koh dah mon-tahn'yah, bah-stoh'nay ahl-pee'noh.

Ice axe, rope. | Piccozza, corda.

pee-kot'sah, korr'dah.

Is there any danger of avalanches ? | C'è pericolo di valanghe ?

chay pay-ree'koh-loh dee vah-lahng'gay ?

Crevasses, glaciers.	Crepacci, ghiacciai.

kray-pahch'chee, ghee-ahch-chah'ee.

Is it advisable to start in this weather ?	E' consigliabile partire con questo tempo ?

ay kon-see-lee-ah'bee-lay pahr-tee'ray kon kwess'toh tem'poh ?

Ascent, descent.	Ascesa (salita), discesa.

ah-shay'zah (sah-lee'tah), dee-shay'zah.

How long will it take to get to the top ?	Quanto ci vorrà per arrivare alla cima ?

kwahn'toh chee vor-rah'pehr ahr-ree-vah'ray ahl'lah chee'mah ?

I am tired.	Sono stanco.

soh'noh stahng'koh.

Let us go on.	Andiamo avanti.

ahn-dee-ah'moh ah-vahn'tee.

We had better go back.	Faremmo meglio a tornare indietro.

fah-rem'moh mayl'yoh ah torr-nah'ray in-dee-ay'troh.

SIGHT-SEEING

See list of " Places of Interest," page 105. A charge is made for admission to all museums, collections, galleries, etc., except on Sundays, when they are open free in the mornings, but remain closed in the afternoons. On Thursdays admission is usually half-price.

Is there a guide here (who can speak English)?	C'è una guida (che parli inglese) ?

chay oo'nah gwee'dah kay pahr'lee eeng-glay'zay ?

Where can I find an interpreter ?	Dove si può trovare un interprete ?

doh'vay see poo-oh' troh-vah'ray oon in-tehr'pray-tay ?

How much do you charge per hour (per day) ?	Quanto chiede all'ora (al giorno) ?

kwahn'toh kee-ay'day ahl-lor'rah (ahl jorr'noh) ?

I don't want a guide.	Non mi occorre una guida.

non mee ock-kor'ray oo'nah gwee'dah.

Is the museum (castle, park) open ?	E' aperto il museo (castello, parco) ?

ay ah-pehr'toh eel moo-zay'oh (kah-stell'loh, pahr'koh) ?

How much is the admission?	Quanto costa l'ingresso ?

kwahn'toh koss'tah lin-gress'soh ?

Where is the entrance (exit) ?	Dov'è l'ingresso (l'uscita) ?

doh-vay' lin-gress'soh (loo-shee'tah) ?

Is one allowed to take photos ?	E'permesso fare foto- grafie ?

ay pehr-mess'soh fah'ray foh-toh-grah-fee'ay ?

MOTORING

The formalities for taking a car to the Continent can be done in England through the A.A. (Automobile Association) or the R.A.C. (Royal Automobile Club). The necessary documents are :

The Triptyque or the Carnet des Passages en Douane.

The International Travelling Pass (Certificato internazionale di via). Drivers should also carry with them their own driving licence. The Touring Club Italiano assists foreign motorists in connection with formalities required in Italy (registration of cars bought in Italy, etc.). This association also supplies good maps on various scales (Atlante Stradale, Carta Automobilistica, Guda delle Strade di Grande Communicazione, etc.). Foreign cars entering Italy may use the Italian roads for three months without paying any tax. After that they become liable to a road-tax (Tassa di circolazione, tahs'sah dee cheer-koh-laht-see-oh'nay), which is payable when they eventually leave the country. Foreign motorists who become members of the A.C.I. (Automobile Club Italiano) are entitled to park their cars in any public car-park (posteggio, poss-ted'joh) free of charge, whereas the ordinary parking charge is 100 liras.

The A.C.I. issues a "Bollettino" (boll-let-tee'noh) every three months, which contains much valuable information for the foreign motorist.

In Italy all vehicles drive on the right side of the road.

ROAD SIGNS

On main roads directions to motorists are as a rule given by means of signs of international meaning. The following is a list of the more useful inscriptions found on less important roads.

Rallentare. Veicoli a passo d'uomo.	Slow !
rahl-len-tah'ray. vay-ee'koh-lee ah pahs'soh doo-oh'moh.	
Alt.	Stop !
ahlt.	
Passaggio a livello.	Level crossing.
pahs-sahd'joh ah lee-vell'loh.	
Svolta pericolosa.	Dangerous bend.
svoll'tah pay-ree-koh-loh'zah.	
Incrocio pericoloso.	Dangerous crossing.
in-kroh'choh pay-ree-koh-loh'zoh.	
Interruzione.	Road up.
in-tehr-root-see-oh'nay.	

PETROL AND OIL

Petrol (benzina, bend-zee'nah) is sold by the litre (1¾ pints), and where there is no petrol pump it is supplied in cans (stagnoni) containing 17 litres or 3¾ gallons. It is easily obtainable and is of two qualities, " super " and ordinary. English cars usually run best when the two qualities are mixed. Oil is sold by the kilo.

Petrol pump.	Distributore di benzina.
dee-stree-boo-tor'ray dee bend-zee'nah.	
I want some petrol (oil).	Ho bisogno di benzina (di olio).
oh bee-zohn'yoh dee bend-zee'nah (dee oll'ee-oh).	
How much per litre (per can) ?	Quanto al litro (allo stagnone) ?
kwahn'toh ahl lee'troh (ahl'loh stæhn-yoh'nay) ?	

AT THE GARAGE

I want to garage the car for the night.	Vorrei mettere la macchina in garage per stanotte.

Vor-ray'ee met'tay-ray lah mahk'kee-nah in gah-radj'pehr stah-not'tay.

Is there a garage here? | C'è qui un garage (una rimessa)?

chay kwee oon gah-radj' (oo'nah ree-mess'sah)?

Will you wash the car? | Può lavare la macchina?

poo-oh' lah-vah'ray lah mahk'kee-nah?

I must leave to-morrow early. | Devo partire domani mattina di buon'ora.

day'voh pahr-tee'ray doh-mah'nee maht-tee'nah dee boo-ohn-or'rah.

Is the garage open all night? | Il garage è aperto tutta la notte?

eel gah-radj' ay ah-pehr'toh toot'tah lah not'tay?

REPAIRS

I have had a breakdown. | Ho avuto un guasto alla macchina.

oh ah-voo'toh oon gwah'stoh ahl'lah mahk'kee-nah.

My car is on the road some kilometres from here. | La mia macchina è sulla strada a qualche chilometro da qui.

lah mee'ah mahk'kee-nah ay sool'lah strah'dah ah kwahl'kay kee-loh'may-troh dah kwee.

Can you send someone there? | Può mandarci qualcuno?

poo-oh' mahn-dahr'chee kwahl-koo'noh?

Can you take me in tow? | Può prendermi a rimorchio?

poo-oh' pren'dehr-mee ah ree-morr'kee-oh?

Do you do repairs? | Fa riparazioni?

fah ree-pah-rath-see-oh'nee?

Can you repair this? | Può riparare questo?

poo-oh' ree-pah-rah'ray kwess'toh?

Can you replace (straighten) this? | Può cambiare (raddrizzare) questo?

poo-oh' kahm-bee-ah'ray (rahd-dreet-sah'ray) kwess'toh?

I have punctured a tyre. | Ho forato una gomma.

oh foh-rah'toh oo'nah gom'mah.

How long shall I have to wait?	Quanto dovrò aspettare?

kwahn'toh doh-vroh' ah-spet-tah'ray?

The sparking plug is sooted up.	La candela è sporca.

lah kahn-day'lah ay sporr'kah.

The engine misfires.	Il motore perde dei colpi.

eel moh-tor'ray pehr'day day'ee koll'pee.

The engine is knocking.	Il motore picchia in testa.

eel moh-tor'ray peek'kee-ah in tess'tah.

The —— doesn't work well.	—— non funziona bene.

. . . non foont-see-oh'nah bay'nay.

There is a leak in the ——.	C'è una perdita nel ——.

chay oo'nah pehr'dee-tah nell . .

VOCABULARY OF MOTOR PARTS

The engine. The accumulator.	Il motore. L'accumulatore.

eel moh-tor'ray. lahk-koo-moo-lah-tor'ray.

The carburettor. The clutch.	Il carburatore. La frizione.

eel kahr-boo-rah-tor'ray. lah freet-see-oh'nay.

The crank shaft. The crank chamber.	L'albero a gomiti. La base del motore.

lahl'bay-roh ah goh'mee-tee. lah bah'zay dell moh-tor'ray.

The cylinder.	Il cilindro.

eel chee-leen'droh.

The exhaust.	Lo scappamento.

loh skahp-pah-men'toh.

The jet.	Lo spruzzatore (Il gicleur).

loh sproot-sah-tor'ray (eel jee-klehr').

The magneto.	Il magnete.

eel mahn-yay'tay.

The sparking plug, the speed gear.	La candela, il cambio di velocità.

lah kahn-day'lah, eel kahm'bee-oh dee vay-loh-chee-tah'.

The radiator, the steering wheel.	Il radiatore, il volante.

eel rah-dee-ah-tor'ray, eel voh-lahn'tay.

The bonnet, the brakes.	Il cofano i freni.

eel koh'fah-noh, ee fray'nee.

The hood.	La capote.

lah kah-pott'.

The headlights, the lamps.	I fari, i fanali.

ee fah'ree, ee fah-nah'lee.

The tail light.	Il fanalino posteriore.

eel fah-nah-lee'noh poss-tay-ree-or'ray.

The mudguards, the springs.	I parafanghi, le molle.

ee pah-rah-fahng'ghee, lay moll'lay.

The tank (is full, empty).	Il serbatoio (è pieno, è vuoto).

eel sehr-bah-toh'yoh (ay pee-ay'noh, ay voo-oh'toh).

The tyres.	Le gomme

lay gom'may.

The cover, the tube.	Il copertone, la camera d'aria.

eel koh-pehr-toh'nay, lah kah'may-rah dah'ree-ah.

TOOLS

Can you lend me ——?	Può imprestarmi ——?

poo-oh' im-press-tahr'mee . . . ?

A spanner, screwdriver.	Una chiave, un cacciavite.

oo'nah kee-ah'vay, oon kahch-chah vee'tay ?

To screw, to unscrew.	Avvitare, svitare.

ahv-vee-tah'ray, svee-tah'ray.

The wrench.	La chiave inglese.

lah kee-ah'vay eeng-glay'zay.

A bolt, nut, washer.	Un bullone, un dado, una rondella.

oon bool-loh'nay, oon dah'doh, oo'nah ron-dell'lah.

The tyre pump. | La pompa.
lah pom'pah.

The jack. | Il cric (il martinetto).
eel kreek (eel mahr-tee-net'toh).

DRIVING

To drive. Start ! Stop ! | Guidare. Parta ! Fermi !
| (Alt !)
gwee-dah'ray. pahr'tah ! fehr'mee ! ahlt !

(Turn) to the right, left. | (Volti) a destra, a sinistra.
(voll'tee) ah dess'trah, ah see-nee'strah.

Go on, go ahead. | Vada avanti, vada diritto.
vah'dah ah-vahn'tee, vah'dah dee-reet'toh.

Go back, reverse. | (Marcia) indietro.
(mahr'chah) in-dee-ay'troh.

Don't go so fast. | Non vada così presto.
non vah'dah koh-zee' press'toh.

Go faster, please. | Più presto, per favore.
pee-oo' press'toh, pehr fah-vor'ray.

At full speed, at a low | A tutta velocità, a
  speed. | piccola velocità.
ah toot'tah vay-loh-chee-tah', ah peek'koh-lah vay-loh-
chee-tah'.

HIRING A CAR

I want to hire a car. | Desidero noleggiare una
| macchina.
day-zee'day-roh noh-led-jah'ray oo'nah mahk'kee-nah.

An open (closed) car. | Una vettura aperta
| (chiusa).
oo'nah vet-too'rah ah-pehr'tah (kee-oo'zah).

A saloon, a touring car. | Una berlina, una
| torpedo.
oo'nah behr-lee'nah, oo'nah torr-pay doh.

How much is it for the | Quanto è al giorno ?
  day ? |
kwahn'toh ay ahl jorr'noh ?

How much per hour (per kilometre) ? | Quanto all'ora (al chilometro) ?
kwahn'toh ah-lor'rah (ahl kee-loh'may-troh) ?

We are going to ——. | Vogliamo andare a ——.
voll-yah'moh ahn-dah'ray ah . . .

We are going to lunch here. | Faremo colazione qui.
fah-ray'moh koh-laht-see-oh'nay kwee.

You will pick us up at —— (at —— o'clock). | Ci venga a prendere a —— (alle ——).
chee veng'gah ah pren'day-ray ah . . . (ahl'lay . . .).

Put the hood up. | Tiri su la capote.
tee'ree soo lah kah-pott'.

PUBLIC ANNOUNCEMENTS

Avviso. | Notice.
ahv-vee'zoh.

(È) proibito (vietato) —. | —— forbidden.
ay proh-ee-bee'toh (vee-ay-tah'toh).

Vietato fumare (sputare). | No smoking (spitting).
vee-ay-tah'toh foo-mah'ray (spoo-tah'ray).

Entrata libera ; ingresso libero. | No charge for admittance.
en-trah'tah lee'bay-rah, in-gress'soh lee'bay-roh.

Vietato l'ingresso. | No admittance.
vee-ay-tah'toh lin-gress'soh.

Fermata (obbligatoria, facoltativa). | Compulsory stop ; stop on request.
fehr-mah'tah (ob-blee-gah-tor'ree-ah, fah-koll-tah-tee'vah).

(Si prega di) non toccare. | (Please) do not touch.
(see pray'gah dee) non tock-kah'ray.

Vernice fresca ; verniciato di fresco. | Fresh paint.
vehr-nee'chay fress'kah ; vehr-nee-chah'toh dee fress'koh.

Suonare. | Ring the bell.
soo-oh-nah'ray.

Riservato ai (soli) pedoni. | Pedestrians only.
ree-zehr-vah'toh ah'ee (soh'lee) pay-doh'nee.

Vietato l'accesso ai veicoli.	One-way street.
vee-ay-tah'toh lahch-chess'soh ah'ee vay-ee'koh-lee.	
Senso proibito.	No traffic in this direction.
sen'soh proh-ee-bee'toh.	
Vietato invertire la di-rezione di marcia.	No reversing.
vee-ay-tah'toh in-vehr-tee'ray lah dee-ret-see-oh'nay dee mahr'chah.	
Vietato il transito.	Closed to traffic.
vee-ay-tah'toh eel trahn'zee-toh.	
Divieto di passaggio.	No thoroughfare.
dee-vee-ay'toh dee pahs-sahd'joh.	
Zona di silenzio.	No hooting.
zoh'nah dee see-lent'see-oh.	
Divieto di sosta ; vietata la sosta (da questo lato).	No parking (on this side).
dee-vee-ay'toh dee soss'tah ; vee-ay-tah'tah lah soss'tah (dah kwess'toh lah'toh).	
Posteggio.	Car-park.
poss-ted'joh.	
Da affittare ; appigio nasi ; est locanda (in Rome).	To be let.
dah ahf-feet-tah'ray ; ahp-pee-joh'nah-see ; est loh-kahn'dah.	
Appartamento ammo-biliato ; camere am-mobiliate.	Furnished flat ; furnished rooms.
ahp-pahr-tah-men'toh ahm-moh-bee-lee-ah'toh ; kah'may-ray ahm-moh-bee-lee-ah'tay.	
Pensione.	Boarding-house.
pen-see-oh'nay.	
Uomini. Donne (Signore).	Gentlemen. Ladies.
oo-oh'mee-nee. don'nay (seen-yor'ray).	
Albergo Diurno.	
ahl-behr'goh dee-oor'noh.	

Buildings so-called are to be found in all Italian towns of any size. They contain lavatories, baths of all kinds, barbers' shops and many other conveniences, and are usually clean and well-kept.

Aperto. Chiuso.	Open. Closed.

ah-pehr'toh. kee-oo'zoh.

Libero. Occupato.	Free. Engaged.

lee'bay-roh. ock-koo-pah'toh.

Riservato.,	Reserved.

ree-zehr-vah'toh.

Riposo.	No performance, closed (theatres).

ree-poh'zoh.

POLICE

Police station.	Questura, Commissariato di P.S.

kwess-too'rah. kom-mees-sah-ree-ah'toh dee poob'blee-
kah see-koo-ret'sah.

*The " Questura " is the central police station in the principal
towns. P.S. is the abbreviation used on signs for " Pubblica
Sicurezza " (public security).*

Policemen.	Guardie; Vigili, Carabinieri.

gwahr'dee-ay. vee'jee-lee. kah-rah-bee-nee-ay'ree.

*" Guardie" "Vigili" are to be found only in towns. "Carabinieri"
or gendarmes are in both town and country. " Metropolitani "
(may-troh-poh-lee-tah'nee) are a special police for Rome only.*

I have come to register myself.	Vengo a fare la dichiarazione di soggiorno,

Veng'goh ah fah'ray lah dee-kee-ah-raht-see-oh'nay dee
sod-jorr'noh.

Here is my passport.	Ecco il mio passaporto.

eck'koh eel mee'oh pass-sah-porr'toh.

My father's (my mother's) name is ——.	Il nome di mio padre (di mia madre) è——.

eel noh'may dee mee'oh pah'dray (dee mee'ah mah'dray)
ay . . .

I arrived yesterday (day before yesterday).	Sono arrivato ieri (ieri l'altro).

soh'noh ahr-ree-vah'toh ee-ay'ree (ee-ay'ree lahl'troh).

I am staying at ——.	Abito a ——.

ah'bee-toh ah . . .

I shall stay here (in Italy) not more than a week.	Mi fermerò qui (in Italia) non più di una settimana.

mee fehr-may-roh′kwee (in ee-tah′lee-ah) non pee-oo′dee oo′nah set-tee-mah′nah.

One month, two months.	Un mese, due mesi.

oon may′zay, doo′ay may′zee.

LOST PROPERTY

I have lost ——.	Ho perduto (smarrito) ——

oh pehr-doo′toh (smahr-ree′toh) . . .

I have been robbed.	Sono stato derubato.

soh′noh stah′toh day-roo-bah′toh.

Will you telephone to me if it is found ?	Se venisse ritrovato vorrebbe telefonarmi ?

say vay-nees′say ree-troh-vah′toh vor-reb′bay tay-lay-foh-nahr′mee ?

GENERAL DIFFICULTIES

I am in difficulties.	Mi trovo in difficoltà.

mee troh′voh in deef-fee-koll-tah′.

What do you call this ?	Come si chiama questo ?

koh′may see kee-ah′mah kwess′toh ?

I don't understand you.	Non La capisco.

non lah kah-pee′skoh.

Do you speak English ?	Parla inglese ?

pahr′lah eeng-glay′zay ?

I cannot speak Italian.	Non so parlare italiano.

non soh pahr-lah′ray ee-tah-lee-ah′noh.

Please speak slowly.	Per favore, parli adagio.

pehr fah-vor′ray, pahr′lee ah-dah′joh.

Is there any one here who can speak English ?	C'e qualcuno qui che parli l'inglese ?

chay kwahl-koo′noh kwee kay pahr′lee leeng-glay′zay ?

Please write it down.	Per favore, me lo scriva.

pehr fah-vor′ray, may loh skree′vah.

English	Italian
Wait a moment, please.	Aspetti un momento, per favore.

ah-spet'tee oon moh-men'toh, pehr fah-vor'ray.

| I cannot pay now. | Non posso pagare ora. |

non poss'soh pah-gah'ray or'rah.

| I have no money left. | Non ho più danaro. |

non oh pee-oo' dah-nah'roh.

| Would you wire for me to my family (to my friends) ? | Vorrebbe telegrafare per me alla mia famiglia (ai miei amici) ? |

vor-reb'bay tay-lay-grah-fah'ray pehr may ahl'lah mee'ah fah-mee'lee-ah (ah'ee mee-ay'ee ah-mee'chee) ?

| This is the address. | Questo è l'indirizzo. |

kwess'toh ay lin-dee-reet'soh.

| Can you wait till next week ? | Può aspettare sino alla prossima settimana ? |

poo-oh' ah-spet-tah'ray see'noh ahl'lah pross'see-mah set-tee-mah'nah ?

| I ought to receive a money order in a few days. | Devo ricevere un vaglia tra pochi giorni. |

day'voh ree-chay'vay-ray oon vah'lee-ah trah poh'kee jorr'nee.

| What is the matter ? | Che cosa c'è ? |

kay koh'zah chay ?

| What has happened ? | Che cosa è successo ? |

kay koh'zah ay sooch-chess'soh ?

| What do you want ? | Che cosa vuole ? |

kay koh'zah voo-oh'lay ?

| Who are you ? | Chi è Lei ? |

kee ay lay'ee ?

| I don't know you. | Io non La conosco. |

ee'oh non lah koh-noss'koh.

| I don't want to speak to you. | Non intendo parlare con Lei. |

non in-ten'doh pahr-lah'ray kon lay'ee.

| Don't bother me ! | Non mi secchi ! |

non mee seck'kee !

| Go away ! | Vada via ! |

vah'dah vee'ah !

I will give you nothing.	Non Le do nulla.
	non lay doh nool'lah.
That will do.	Ora basta.
	or'rah bah'stah.
You are mistaken.	Lei si sbaglia.
	lay'ee see sbahl'yah.
It was not I.	Non sono stato io.
	non soh'noh stah'toh ee'oh.
What have I done ?	Che cosa ho fatto ?
	kay koh'zah oh faht'toh ?
I have done nothing.	Non ho fatto nulla.
	non oh faht'toh nool'lah.
It was not my fault.	Non è stata colpa mia.
	non ay stah'tah koll'pah mee'ah.
I did not know it.	Non lo sapevo.
	non loh sah-pay'voh.
I did not do it on purpose.	Non l'ho fatto apposta.
	non loh faht'toh ahp-poss'tah.
I shall call a policeman.	Ora chiamo una guardia.
	or'rah kee-ah'moh oo'nah gwahr'dee-ah.
Bring a policeman.	Faccia venire una guardia.
	fahch'chah vay-nee'ray oo'nah gwahr'dee-ah.
Help !	Aiuto !
	ah-yoo'toh !
This man is following me everywhere.	Quest'uomo mi segue dappertutto.
	kwess-too-oh'moh mee say'gway dahp-pehr-toot'toh.
Someone has robbed me.	Qualcuno mi ha derubato.
	kwahl-koo'noh mee ah day-roo-bah'toh.
That man (that woman).	Quell'uomo (quella donna).
	kwell-loo-oh'moh (kwell'lah don'nah).
I want to see the British Consul.	Voglio parlare con il console inglese.
	voll'yoh pahr-lah'ray kon eel kon'soh-lay eeng-glay'zay.
Where is the British Consulate ?	Dov'è il consolato britannico ?
	doh-vay' eel kon-soh-lah'toh bree-tahn'nee-koh ?

CONVERSATION : VISITING : RECREATION

COMMON WORDS AND PHRASES

Yes, No.	Si, No.

see, no(r).

Please, Thank you,	Per favore, Grazie,
Thank you so much.	Grazie tanté.

pehr fah-vor'ray, graht'see-ay, graht'see-ay tahn'tay.

Don't mention it.	Prego.

pray'goh.

Excuse me.	Scusi.

skoo'zee.

Bring me ——, Give me —.	Mi porti ——, Mi dia —.

mee porr'tee. mee dee'ah.

Good-morning (after-	Buon giorno.
noon). Good-day.	

boo-ohn' jorr'noh.

Good-evening, madam.	Buona sera, signora.[1]

boo-oh'nah say'rah, seen-yor'rah.

Good-night.	Buona sera (buona
	notte).

boo-oh'nah say'rah (boo-oh'nah not'tay).

Good-bye.	Arrivederla.

ahr-ree-vay-dehr'lah.

How do you do ?	Come sta ?

koh'may stah ?

Very well, thank you ;	Benissimo, grazie ; e
and you ?	Lei ?

bay-nees'see-moh, graht'see-ay ; ay lay'ee ?

Have you ——? How	Ha ——? Quanto ?
much ?	

ah ? . . . kwahn'toh ?

---

[1] *The Italians generally use Signor* (seen'yorr), *Mr. ——,*
Signora, Mrs.——, and Signorina (seen-yor-ree'nah), *Miss ——,*
in speaking to people, without adding any name (cf. similar
custom in France).

I am glad, I am sorry. | Sono lieto, mi dispiace.
soh-noh lee-ay′toh, mee dee-spee-ah′chay.

I like this very much. | Questo mi piace assai.
kwess′toh mee pee-ah′chay ahs-sah′ee.

I am in a hurry. | Ho fretta.
oh fret′tah.

It is late (early). | E′ tardi (presto).
ay tahr′dee (press′toh).

What is the time ? | Che ora è ?   Che ore sono ?
kay or′rah ay ?   kay or′ray soh′noh ?

What do you say ? | Che cosa dice ?
kay koh′zah dee′chay ?

I did not understand; do you mind repeating ? | Non ho capito ; Le dispiace ripetere ?
non oh kah-pee′toh ; lay dee-spee-ah′chay ree-pay′tay-ray ?

What does that mean ? | Che cosa vuol dire ?
kay koh′zah voo-ohl′dee′ray ?

What is that for ? | A che serve ?
ah kay sehr′vay ?

What is your name? (What is it called ?) | Come si chiama ?
koh′may see kee-ah′mah ?

What is your address ? | Qual′è il Suo indirizzo ?
kwah-lay′eel soo′oh in-dee-reet′soh ?

Where are you going ? | Dove va ?
doh′vay vah ?

How soon will you be back ? | Fra quanto torna ?
frah kwahn′toh torr′nah ?

Why ? | Perchè ?
pehr-kay′ ?

How ? | Come ?
koh′may ?

ON THE TELEPHONE

In most towns the telephone is now entirely on the automatic system. To call a subscriber in the same town simply dial the five or six figures of which his number is composed.

TRUNK CALL *charges cover a conversation of three minutes, as in England, but after three minutes the operator ("* la signorina," *lah seen-yor-ree'nah) breaks in asking : "* Rad-doppia ? " *(rahd-dopp'yah ?), i.e., "Will you pay double charge ?" If the caller wishes to continue the conversation he must answer : "* Raddoppio ! " *(rahd-dopp'yoh !). On Sundays the charges for trunk calls in Italy are reduced to one-half.*

*To use public telephones, callers must put a metal token (*gettone, *jet-toh'nay) in the slot. They can be bought at the counter in the post office or shop for 20 liras. Trunk calls can only be made from special offices.*

Where may I telephone ?	Dove posso telefonare ?
	doh'vay poss'soh tay-lay-foh-nah'ray ?
Have you a directory ?	Ha un elenco telefonico ?
	ah oon ay-leng'koh tay-lay-foh'nee-koh ?
Give me a token, please.	Mi dia un gettone, per favore.
	mee dee'ah oon jet-toh'nay, pehr fah-vor'ray.
Hallo !	Pronto !
	pron'toh !
Who is speaking ?	Chi parla ? Con chi parlo ?
	kee pahr'lah ? kon kee pahr'loh ?
Can I speak to —— ?	Posso parlare con —— ?
	poss'soh pahr-lah'ray kon . . . ?
This is —— speaking.	Parla ——.
	pahr'lah . . .
I will ring you up later.	Le telefonerò più tardi.
	lay tay-lay-foh-nay-roh' pee-oo' tahr'dee.
Ring me up.	Mi telefoni.
	mee tay-lay'foh-nee.
My number is ——.	Il mio numero è ——.
	eel mee'oh noo'may-roh ay . . .
Trunk call service.	Intercomunale.
	in-tehr-koh-moo-nah'lay.

VISITING FRIENDS

Does Mr. (Mrs.) —— live here ?	Il signor (la signora) — abita qui ?

eel seen-yorr' (lah seen-yor'rah) . . . ah'bee-tah kwee ?

Is he (she) at home ?	E' in casa ?

ay in kah'zah ?

When will he (she) be in ?	Quando sarà in casa ?

kwahn'doh sah-rah' in kah'zah ?

I am ——.	Il mio nome è ——.

eel mee'oh noh'may ay , . .

Here is my card.	Ecco il mio biglietto.

eck'koh eel mee'oh beel-yet'toh.

I have a letter for you from ——.	Ho una lettera per Lei da ——.

oh oo'nah let'tay-rah pehr lay'ee dah . . .

Mr. —— asked me to look you up.	Il Signor —— mi pregò di venirla a trovare.

eel seen-yorr' —— mee pray-goh' dee vay-neer'lah ah troh-vah'ray.

He sends you his kind regards.	Le manda i suoi saluti.

lay mahn'dah ee soo-oh'ee sah-loo'tee.

How do you do ?	Come sta ?

koh'may stah ?

Let me introduce my wife (husband).	Permetta che Le presenti mia moglie (mio marito).

pehr-met'tah kay lay pray-zen'tee mee'ah mohl'yay (mee'oh mah-ree'toh).

My son (daughter).	Mio figlio (mia figlia).

mee'oh feel'yoh (mee'ah feel'yah).

My uncle (aunt).	Mio zio (mia zia).

mee'oh tsee'oh (mee'ah tsee'ah).

My nephew (niece).	Mio nipote (mia nipote).

mee'oh nee-poh'tay (mee'ah nee-poh'tay).

| Delighted to meet you. | Fortunatissimo (di fare la Sua conoscenza). |

forr-too-nah-tees'see-moh (dee fah'ray lah soo'ah koh-noh-
shent'sah).

| I am sorry I cannot speak Italian. | Mi dispiace di non saper parlare italiano. |

mee dee-spee-ah'chay dee non sah-pehr' pahr-lah'ray
ee-tah-lee-ah'noh.

| I am in Italy for the first time. | E' la prima volta che vengo in Italia. |

ay lah pree'mah voll'tah kay veng'goh in ee-tah'lee-ah.

| I like it very much. | Mi piace molto. |

mee pee-ah'chay moll'toh.

| (I am) so glad to have met you. | (Sono) lietissimo di averla conosciuta. |

(soh'noh) lee-ay-tees'see-moh dee ah-vehr'lah koh-noh-
shoo'tah.

| Thank you very much. | Grazie mille. |

graht'see-ay meel'lay.

| When shall I see you again ? | Quando potrò rivederla ? |

kwahn'doh poh-troh' ree-vay-dehr'lah ?

| Good-bye. | Arrivederla. |

ahr-ree-vay-dehr'lah.

THEATRES, ETC.

| Where can I spend the evening ? | Dove posso passare la serata ? |

doh'vay poss'soh pass-sah'ray lah say-rah'tah ?

| Opera, opera season, concert. | Opera, stagione lirica, concerto. |

oh'pay-rah, stah-joh'nay lee'ree-kah, kon-chehr'toh.

| The theatre, the music hall. | Il teatro, il varietà. |

eel tay-ah'troh, eel vah-ree-ay-tah'.

| The cinema. | Il cinematografo. |

eel chee-nay-mah-toh'grah-foh.

Is there a matinée to-day ? | C'è matinée oggi ?
chay mah-tee-nay' od'jee ?

At what time does the performance start ? | A che ora comincia la rappresentazione ?
ah kay or'rah koh-meen'chah lah rahp-pray-zen-taht-see-oh' nay ?

When will it be over ? | Quando terminerà ?
kwahn'doh tehr-mee nay-rah' ?

What should I wear ? | Come mi devo vestire ?
koh'may mee day'voh vess-tee'ray ?

The cloakroom. | Il guardaroba.
eel gwahr-dah-roh'bah.

The box office. | La biglietteria.
lah beel-yet-tay-ree'ah.

Have you any seats for this evening ? | Ci sono posti per stasera ?
chee soh'noh poss'tee pehr stah-say'rah ?

Orchestra stalls. | Poltrone. Poltroncine.
poll-troh'nay. poll-trohn-chee'nay.

" Poltroncine" are back-row stalls and cost less.

Pit seats. | Posti di platea.
poss'tee dee plah-tay'ah.

Standing-room. | Posti in piedi.
poss'tee in pee-ay'dee.

Dress circle. | Prima galleria (gradinata).
pree'mah gahl-lay-ree'ah (grah-dee-nah'tah).

Upper circle. | Seconda galleria (gradinata).
say-kon'dah gahl-lay-ree'ah (grah-dee-nah'tah).

Gallery. | Loggione.
lod-joh'nay.

Reserved seats. | Posti numerati.
poss'tee noo-may-rah'tee.

A box. | Un palco.
oon pahl'koh.

Admission ticket.	Biglietto d'ingresso.[1]

beel-yet'toh din-gress'soh.

A synchronised film.	Un film sonoro.

oon feelm soh-nor'roh.

A talkie.	Un film parlato.

oon feelm pahr-lah'toh.

I should like to dance.	Vorrei ballare.

vor-ray'ee bahl-lah'ray.

Do you dance ?	Lei balla ?

lay'ee bahl'lah ?

Will you dance with me ?	Vuole ballare con me ?

voo-oh'lay bahl-lah'ray kon may ?

Will you have something to drink (eat) ?	Vuole bere (mangiare) qualche cosa ?

voo-oh'lay bay'ray (mahn-jah'ray) kwahl'kay koh'zah ?

Let us have another dance.	Balliamo ancora.

bahl-lee-ah'moh ahng-kor'rah.

Let us sit down.	Andiamo a sederci.

ahn-dee-ah'moh ah say-dehr'chec.

May I see you home ?	Posso accompagnarla a casa ?

poss'soh ahk-kom-pahn-yahr'lah ah kah'zah ?

BATHING

A seaside resort.	Una stazione balneare.

oo'nah staht-see-oh'nay bahl-nay-ah'ray.

Is there a bathing establishment here ?	C'è uno stabilimento di bagni qui ?

chay oo'noh stah-bee-lee-men'toh dee bahn'yee kwee ?

[1] *Theatre-goers taking a box must also pay for separate admission tickets.*

Where can I hire a hut ?	Dove si può affittare una cabina ?

doh'vay see poo-oh' ahf-feet-tah'ray oo'nah kah-bee'nah ?

Bathing costume, wrap.	Costume da bagno, accappatoio.

koss-too'may dah bahn'yoh, ahk-kahp-pah-toh'yoh.

High (low) tide, the waves.	Alta (bassa) marea, le onde.

ahl'tah (bahs'sah) mah-ray'ah, lay on'day.

What is the depth here ?	Quanto è profondo qui ?

kwahn'toh ay proh-fon'doh kwee ?

The beach, sand.	La spiaggia, sabbia.

lah spee-ahd'jah, sahb'bee-ah.

A sun bath.	Un bagno di sole.

oon bahn'yoh dee soh'lay.

Beach umbrella.	Ombrellone.

om-brell-loh'nay.

A deck-chair.	Una sedia a sdraio.

oo'nah say'dee-ah ah zdrah'yoh.

Coconut oil.	Olio di cocco.

oll'ee-oh dee kock'koh.

Sun-burn.	Scottature del sole.

skot-tah-too'ray dell soh'lay.

Is it dangerous (allowed) to bathe here ?	E' pericoloso (permesso) fare il bagno qui ?

ay pay-ree-koh·loh'zoh (pehr-mess'soh) fah'ray eel bahn'yoh kwee ?

I cannot swim.	Non so nuotare.

non soh noo-oh-tah'ray.

SPORTS AND GAMES

For most sports (tennis, golf, football, etc.), and some card games (bridge, etc.), the English terms are used and are pronounced as in English.

Lawn tennis is now played practically everywhere in Italy, and even less important towns have their tennis club. In the principal cities and at fashionable holiday resorts there exist golf links. Amongst winter sports, ski-ing has become quite popular in Northern Italy. All kinds of racing are popular, and cycling is a favourite pastime for boys and young men (there are many cycling clubs). Bicycle races rouse the wildest enthusiasm.[1]

Tennis court.	Campo di tennis.
	kahm'poh dee ten'nees.
Golf course.	Campo di golf.
	kahm'poh dee golf.
Tennis racquet.	Racchetta.
	rahk-ket'tah.
Ball.	Palla.
	pahl'lah.
Net.	Rete.
	ray'tay.
Do you play —— ?	Lei gioca a —— ?
	lay'ee joh'kah ah . . . ?
I do not play ——.	Non gioco a ——.
	non joh'koh ah . . .
Football.	calcio.[2]
	kahl'choh.
Football player.	Giocatore di calcio.
	joh-kah-tor'ray dee kahl'choh.
Football ground.	Stadio.
	stah'dee-oh.
Referee.	Arbitro.
	ahr' bee-troh.
Match.	Partita.
	pahr-tee'tah.
Grand-stand.	Tribuna.
	tree-boo'nah.

[1] *One of the greatest sporting events of the year in Italy is the Giro d'Italia (jee'roh dee-tah'lee-ah), which takes place towards the end of May.*

[2] *One of the most interesting sights for the tourist is the Calcio in Costume (kahl'choh in koss-too'may), a football match in seventeenth-century costume, played yearly in Florence on the Feast of Corpus Domini and on St. John's Day.*

Grand-stand seat.	Posto di tribuna.

poss'toh dee tree-boo'nah.

Winter sports.	Sport invernali.

sporrt in-vehr-nah'lee.

To ski.	Sciare.

shee-ah'ray.

Ski, sticks.	Sci, bastoncini.

shee, bah-stohn-chee'nee.

To jump.	Saltare.

sahl-tah'ray.

Downhill race.	Corsa in discesa.

korr'sah in dee-shay'zah.

Snow conditions.	Stato della neve.

stah'toh dell'lah nay'vay.

Sledge.	Slitta.

zleet'tah.

To skate, skates.	Pattinare, pattini.

paht-tee-nah'ray, paht'tee-nee.

Skating-rink.	Pattinatoio.

paht-tee-nah-toh'yoh.

To ride.	Andare a cavallo.

ahn-dah'ray ah kah-vahl'loh.

Riding-school.	Scuola di equitazione.

skoo-oh'lah dee ay-kwee-taht-see-oh'nay.

To hire a horse.	Noleggiare un cavallo.

noh-led-jah'ray oon kah-vahl'loh.

Horse races.	Corse di cavallo.

korr'say dee kah-vahl'loh.

Motor races.	Corse automobilistiche.[1]

korr'say ow-toh-moh-bee-lee'stee-kay.

Motor-cycle trials.	Corse di motocicletta.

korr'say dee moh-toh-chee-klet'tah.

Cycle races.	Corse di bicicletta.

korr'say dee bee-chee-klet'tah.

Prize.	Premio.

pray'mee-oh.

[1] *The most important motor race is the Mille Miglia* (mill'lay meel'yah), *an international race run in April each year.*

| Billiards ; the cue. | Bigliardo ; stecca. |
| beel-yahr′doh ; steck′kah. | |

| Chess ; check ; check-mate. | Scacchi ; scacco ; scaccomatto. |
| skahk′kee ; skahk′koh ; skahk-koh-maht′toh. | |

| Draughts. | Dama. |
| dah′mah. | |

| To play cards ; card games. | Giocare a carte ; giochi di carte. |
| joh-kah′ray ah kahr′tay ; joh′kee dee kahr′tay. | |

| To shuffle, to cut cards. | Mescolare, alzare le carte. |
| mess-koh-lah′ray, ahlt-sah′ray lay kahr′tay. | |

| To deal. | Fare il mazzo. |
| fah′ray eel maht′soh. | |

| Wireless, —— set. | Radio, apparecchio radio. |
| rah′dee-oh, ahp-pah-reck′kee-oh rah′dee-oh. | |

| Loud speaker. | Altoparlante. |
| ahl-toh-pahr-lahn′tay. | |

| Broadcast. | Trasmissione. |
| trahs-mee-see-oh′nay. | |

| What is the broadcasting programme to-night ? | Che programma c'è alla radio stasera ? |
| kay proh-grahm′mah chay ahl′lah rah′dee-oh stah-say′rah ? | |

SHOPPING

CHANGING MONEY : THE BANK

| Is there a bank (a money changer's) near here ? | C'è una banca (un cambiavalute) qui vicino ? |
| chay oo′nah bahng′kah (oon kahm-bee-ah-vah-loo′tay) kwee vee-chee′noh ? | |

| Where can one change money ? | Dove si può cambiare il denaro ? |
| doh′vay see poo-oh′ kahm-bee-ah′ray eel day-nah′roh ? | |

I.   C

| Please change this note (these notes). | Per favore mi cambi questo biglietto (questi biglietti). |

pehr fah-vor'ray, mee kahm'bee kwess'toh beel-yet'toh (kwess'tee beel-yet'tee).

| Can you cash me this cheque ? | Può incassarmi questo cheque (assegno) ? |

poo-oh' in-kahs-sahr'mee kwess'toh check (ahs-sayn'yoh) ?

| What is the rate of exchange (on London) to-day ? | Qual'è il cambio (su Londra) oggi ? |

kwah-lay'eel kahm'bee-oh (soo lon'drah) od'jee ?

| Would you write it down ? | Vuole scrivermelo ? |

voo-oh'lay skree'vehr-may-loh ?

| Give me large notes, please. | Mi dia dei biglietti di grosso taglio, per favore. |

mee dee'ah day'ee beel-yet'tee dee gross'soh tahl'yoh, pehr fah-vor'ray.

| Can you give me small change ? | Mi può dare della moneta (degli spiccioli) ? |

mee poo-oh' dah'ray dell'lah moh-nay'tah (dayl'yee speech'choh-lee) ?

| I have a letter of credit. | Ho una lettera di credito. |

oh oo'nah let'tay-rah dee kray'dee-toh.

| Can I see the manager ? | Posso parlare col direttore ? |

poss'soh pahr-lah'ray koll dee-ret-tor'ray ?

THE POST OFFICE

Postage stamps can be had at any tobacconist's as well as at post offices. Postal rates, for abroad : letters, 55 lire ; post cards, 35 lire (if with sender's signature and with not more than five words of greeting, 8 lire). For Italy : letters, 20 lire ; post cards, 15 lire. It should be noted, however, that these rates are constantly changing.

The general post office.	La posta centrale.

lah poss'tah chen-trah'lay.

The post office.	L'ufficio postale.

loof-fee'choh poss-tah'lay.

Is the post office near here ?	E' vicino l'ufficio postale ?

ay vee-chee'noh loof-fee'choh poss-tah'lay ?

One 20-lire stamp.	Un francobollo da venti.

oon frahng-koh-boll'loh dah ven'tee.

Give me a card for abroad.	Mi dia una cartolina per l'estero.[1]

mee dee'ah oo'nah kahr-toh-lee'nah pehr less'tay-roh.

—— stamps at —— (numerals, p. 98).	—— francobolli da ——.

... frahng-koh-boll'lee dah ...

What is the postage for this letter ?	Quanto è il porto per questa lettera ?

kwahn'toh ay eel porr'toh pehr kwess'tah let'tay-rah ?

The postman, the post official.	Il portalettere (il postino), l'impiegato postale.

eel porr-tah-let'tay-ray (eel poss-tee'noh), lim-pee-ay-gah'toh poss-tah'lay.

The collection, the delivery.	La levata, la distribuzione.

lah lay-vah'tah, lah dee-stree-boot-see-oh'nay.

A telegram, a cablegram.	Un telegramma, un cablogramma.

oon tay-lay-grahm'mah, oon kah-bloh-grahm'mah.

Please give me a telegraph form.	Mi dia per favore un modulo.

mee dee'ah pehr fah-vor'ray oon moh'doo-loh.

A wireless message.	Un marconigramma.

oon mahr-koh-nee-grahm'mah.

---

[1] *Plain post cards are sold ready stamped. No charge is made for the card itself.*

An urgent telegram. | Un telegramma urgente (urgentissimo).

oon tay-lay-grahm'mah oor-jen'tay (oor-jen-tees'see-moh).

" Telegrammi urgenti " (tay-lay-grahm'mee oor-jen'tee) *cost twice the ordinary rate ; " urgentissimi "* (oor-jen-tees'see-mee) *three times as much ; and " telegrammi lampo "* (lahm'poh), *which are delivered within a few minutes of dispatch, about five times as much. Telegrams sent to places within the same province are charged at slightly lower rates.*

A postal order. | Un vaglia postale.

oon vahl'yah poss-tah'lay.

International money order. | Vaglia internazionale.

vahl'yah in-tehr-naht-see-oh-nah'lay.

Telegraphic money order. | Vaglia telegrafico.

vahl'yah tay-lay-grah'fee-koh.

I want to register this letter. | Vorrei raccomandare questa lettera.

vor-ray'ee rahk-koh-mahn-dah'ray kwesss'tah let'tay-rah.

Parcel post. | Pacco postale.

pahk'koh poss-tah'lay.

THE POSTE RESTANTE

Are there any letters for A—— B——? | Ci sono lettere per A—— B——?

chee soh'noh let'tay-ray pehr . . . ?

Here is my passport. | Ecco il mio passaporto.

eck'koh eel mee'oh pass-sah-porr'toh.

I am leaving for ——. | Parto per ——.

pahr'toh pehr . . .

Will you have any letters for me forwarded there, c/o G.P.O.? | Vuole far proseguire là la mia corrispondenza, fermo posta?

voo-oh'lay fahr proh-say-gwee'ray lah' lah mee'ah kor-ree-spon-dent'sah, fehr'moh poss'tah?

THE TOBACCONIST

Where is there a tobacconist ?	Dove c'è un tabaccaio ?

doh'vay chay oon tah-bahk-kah'yoh ?

I want some tobacco.	Vorrei del tabacco.

vor-ray'ee dell tah-bahk'koh.

Mild (strong) tobacco.	Tabacco leggero (forte).

tah-bahk'koh led-jay'roh (forr'tay).

Have you any English (Swiss) cigarettes ?	Ha sigarette inglesi (svizzere).

ah dell'lay see-gah-ret'tay eeng-glay'zee (sweet'say-ray) ?

How much are these ?	Quanto costano queste ?

kwahn'toh koss'tah-noh kwess'tay ?

I want some cigars.	Vorrei dei sigari.

vor-ray'ee day'ee see'gah-ree.

A packet (a box) of 10, 20.	Un pacchetto (una scatola) di dieci, venti.

oon pahk-ket'toh (oo'nah skah'toh-lah) dee dee-ay'chee, ven'tee.

A box of matches.	Una scatola di fiammiferi.

oo'nah skah'toh-lah dee fee-ahm-mee'fay-ree.

Safety matches.	Svedesi.

svay-day'zee.

Wax matches.	Cerini.

chay-ree'nee.

A pipe, a mouthpiece (a holder), a lighter.	Una pipa, un bocchino, un accenditoio.

oo'nah pee'pah, oon bock-kee'noh, oon ahch-chen-dee-toh'yoh.

Can you give me some petrol for my lighter ?	Mi può dare della benzina per il mio accenditoio ?

mee poo-oh' dah'ray dell'lah bend-zee'nah pehr cel mee'oh ahch-chen-dee-toh'yoh ?

A pack of playing cards.	Un mazzo di carte da giuoco.

oon maht'soh dee kahr'tay dah joh'koh.

THE HAIRDRESSER, THE BARBER

The hairdresser, the barber.	Il parrucchiere (la parrucchiera), il barbiere.

eel pah-rook-kee-ay'ray (lah pah-rook-kee-ay'rah), eel bahr-bee-ay'ray.

I want a haircut.	Mi tagli i capelli.

mee tahl'yee ee kah-pell'lee.

I want a shave.	Mi faccia la barba.

mee fahch'chah lah bahr'bah.

A shave and a haircut.	Barba e capelli.

bahr'bah ay kah-pell'lee.

Don't cut it too short behind (in front).	Non li tagli troppo corti dietro (davanti).

non lee tahl'yee trop'poh korr'tee dee-ay'troh (dah-vahn'tee).

Give me a shampoo (a wave).	Mi faccia uno shampoo (un'ondulazione).

mee fahch'chah oo'noh shahm'poo (oo-non-doo-laht-see-oh'nay).

Permanent wave.	Ondulazione permanente.

on-doo-laht-see-oh'nay pehr-mah-nen'tay.

Moustache, beard.	Baffi, barba.

bahf'fee, bahr'bah.

The comb, the brush.	Il pettine, la spazzola.

eel pet'tee-nay, lah spaht'soh-lah.

Is there a manicurist?	C'è una manicure?

chay oo'nah mah-nee-koo'ray?

I want a manicure.	Vorrei farmi le mani.

vor-ray'ee fahr'mee lay mah'nee.

I want to make an appointment.	Vorrei fare un appuntamento.

vor-ray'ee fah'ray oon ahp-poon-tah-men'toh.

THE CHEMIST

Can you recommend me a chemist's where they speak English?	Può indicarmi una farmacia dove parlino inglese?

poo-oh' in-dee-kahr'mee oo'nah fahr-mah-chee'ah doh'vay pahr'lee-noh eeng-glay'zay?

Can you make up this prescription ?	Può prepararmi questa ricetta ?

poo-oh' pray-pah-rahr'mee kwess'tah ree-chet'tah ?

When shall I come back?	Quando devo tornare ?

kwahn'doh day'voh torr-nah'ray ?

Can you recommend a good doctor (surgeon, specialist) ?	Può indicarmi un buon medico (chirurgo, specialista) ?

poo-oh' in-dee-kahr'mee oon boo-ohn' may'dee-koh (kee-roor'goh, spay-chah-lee'stah) ?

Can you get me a trained nurse ?	Mi può procurare una brava infermiera ?

mee poo-oh' proh-koo-rah'ray oo'nah brah'vah in-fehr-mee-ay'rah ?

Is there a hospital (nursing home) ?	C'è uno spedale (una clinica) ?

chay oo'noh spay-dah'lay (oo'nah klee'nee-kah) ?

I feel faint, over-tired.	Mi sento debole, spossato.

mee sen'toh day'boh-lay (sposs-sah'toh).

I feel giddy, feverish.	Mi gira la testa, ho la febbre.

mee jee'rah lah tess'tah, oh lah feb'bray.

I have toothache (ear-ache, stomachache).	Ho mal di denti (d'orecchie, di pancia).

oh mahl'dee den'tee (dor-reck'kee-ay, dee pahn'chah).

I have a headache.	Ho mal di testa.

oh mahl'dee tess'tah.

I have a sore throat.	Ho mal di gola.

oh mahl dee goh'lah.

Bandages, boric acid.	Bende, acido borico.

ben'day, ah'chee-doh bor'ree-koh.

Carbolic acid.	Acido fenico.

ah'chee-doh fay'nee-koh.

Castor oil.	Olio di ricino.

oll'yoh dee ree'chee-noh.

Collyrium, corn pads.	Collirio, cerotti per i calli.

koll-lee'ree-oh, chay-rot'tee pehr ee kahl'lee.

Cotton wool. | Cotone idrofilo.
koh-toh'nay ee-droh'fee-loh.

Gargle, gauze. | Gargarismo, garza.
gahr-gah-reez'moh, gahrd'zah.

Iodine (tincture). | Tintura di iodio.
teen-too'rah dee yoh'dee-oh.

Nail brush. | Spazzolino per le unghie.
spaht-soh-lee'noh pehr lay oong'ghee-ay.

Poultice. | Impacco.
im-pahk'koh.

Purge, quinine. | Purga, chinino.
poor'gah, kee-nee'noh.

Sanitary towels. | Assorbenti igienici.
ahs-sorr-ben'tee ee-jay'nee-chee.

Smelling salts. | Sali d'ammoniaca.
sah'lee dahm-moh-nee'ah-kah.

Soap, sticking-plaster. | Sapone, cerotto.
sah-poh'nay, chay-rot'toh.

Sun-burn ointment. | Pomata per le scottature
del sole.
poh-mah'tah pehr lay skot-tah-too'ray dell soh'lay.

Talcum powder. | Polvere di talco.
poll'vay-ray dee tahl'koh.

Throat pastilles. | Pastiglie (pasticche) per
la gola.
pah-steel'yay (pah-steek'kay) pehr lah goh'lah.

Toilet paper. | Carta igienica.
kahr'tah ee-jay'nee-kah.

Vaseline. | Vaselina.
vah-zay-lee'nah.

PHOTOGRAPHY

Dark room. | Camera oscura.
kah'may-rah oss-koo'rah.

I want some films (plates) | Vorrei delle pellicole (lastre)
for my camera. | per la mia macchina.
vor-ray'ee dell'lay pell-lee'koh-lay (lah'stray) pehr lah
mee'ah mahk'kee-nah.

Do you develop films ? | Sviluppa fotografie ?
svee-loop'pah foh-toh-grah-fee'ay ?

How much do you charge for developing a roll (for each print) ? | Quanto prende per sviluppare un rotolo (per ogni copia) ?
kwahn'toh pren'day pehr svee-loop-pah'ray oon roh'toh-loh (pehr on'yee koh'pee-ah) ?

One print (two prints) of each. | Una copia (due copie) di ciascuna.
oo'nah koh'pee-ah (doo'ay koh'pee-ay) dee chah-skoo'nah).

On shiny (matt) paper. | Su carta lucida (opaca).
soo kahr'tah loo'chee-dah (oh-pah'kah).

When will they be ready ? | Quando saranno pronte ?
kwahn'doh sah-rahn'noh pron'tay ?

My name is ——. | Il mio nome è ——.
eel mee'oh noh'may ay . . .

Are the prints I ordered ready ? | Sono pronte le copie che avevo ordinato ?
soh'noh pron'tay lay koh'pee-ay kay ah-vay'voh orr-dee-nah'toh ?

BOOKSHOP

Where is there a bookshop. | Dov'è una libreria ?
doh-vay' oo'nah lee-bray-ree'ah ?

Have you any English novels (newspapers) ? | Ha romanzi (giornali) inglesi ?
ah roh-mahnd'zee (jorr-nah'lee) eeng-glay'zee ?

Have you any of ——'s books ? | Ha qualche libro di ——?
ah kwahl'kay lee'broh dee . . . ?

In English (Italian). | In inglese (italiano).
in eeng-glay'zay (ee-tah-lee-ah'noh) ?

I want an Italian-English (English-Italian) dictionary. | Desidero un vocabolario italiano-inglese (inglese-italiano).
day-zee'day-roh oon voh-kah-boh-lah'ree-oh ee-tah-lee-ah'noh eeng-glay'zay (eeng-glay'zay ee-tah-lee-ah'noh).

Have you a map of Italy | Ha una carta d'Italia
  (of the district) ? | (della regione) ?
ah oo'nah kahr'tah dee-tah'lee-ah (dell'lah ray-joh'nay) ?

A plan of the town. | Una pianta della città.
oo'nah pee-ahn'tah dell'lah chit-tah' ?

A guide to this town. | Una guida della città.
oo'nah gwee'dah dell'lah chit-tah' ?

STATIONER

Stationer. | Cartolaio.
kahr-toh-lah'yoh.

Some writing paper, | Della carta da lettere,
  envelopes. | delle buste.
dell'lah kahr'tah dah let'tay-ray, dell'lay boo'stay.

Picture post-cards. | Cartoline illustrate.
kahr-toh-lee'nay eel-loo-strah'tay.

A pen, a pencil. | Una penna, una matita,
  | (un lapis).
oo'nah pen'nah, oo'nah mah-tee'tah (oon lah'piss).

A bottle of ink, pen nibs. | Una boccetta d'inchio-
  | stro, dei pennini.
oo'nah boch-chet'tah ding-kee-oss'troh, day'ee pen-nee'nee.

Can you refill my foun- | Può riempire la mia
  tain pen ? | penna stilografica ?
poo-oh' ree-em-pee'ray lah mee'ah pen'nah stee-loh-grah'fee-
                        kah ?

CLOTHING

Underwear (lingerie), | Biancheria, maglieria.
  hosiery. |
bee-ahng-kay-ree'ah, mahl-yay-ree'ah.

A shirt. | Una camicia (da uomo).
oo'nah kah-mee'chah (dah oo-oh'moh).

A night-dress. | Una camicia da notte.
oo'nah kah-mee'chah dah not'tay.

A dressing-gown. | Una vestaglia.
oo'nah vess-tahl'yah.

| Pyjamas. | Un pigiama. |

oon pee-jah'mah.

| Vest, combinations. | Magila, pagliacetto |

mahl'yah, pahl-yah-chet'toh.

| Knickers, pants. | Culottes, mutande. |

koo-lott', moo-tahn'day.

| Petticoat, corset, brassière. | Sottabito, busto, reggi- petto. |

sott-tah'bee-toh, boo'stoh, red-jee-pet'toh.

| A pair of socks. | Un paio di calzini. |

oon pah'yoh dee kahlt-see'nee.

| Stockings. | Calze. |

kahlt'say.

| Man's, woman's (lady's). | Da uomo, da donna (signora). |

dah oo-oh'moh, dah don'nah (seen-yor'rah).

| Of wool, cotton, silk, artificial silk. | Di lana, cotone, seta, raion. |

dee lah'nah, koh-toh'nay, say'tah rah-onn'.

| (Linen) handkerchief. | Fazzoletto (di lino). |

faht-soh-let'toh (dee lee'noh).

| Collar, collar stud. | Colletto, bottone da collo. |

koll-let'toh, bot-toh'nay dah koll'loh.

| Garters, braces, suspenders. | Giarrettiere, bretelle, reggicalze. |

jahr-ret-tee-ay'ray, bray-tell'lay, red-jee-kahlt'say.

| A suit of clothes. | Un abito completo. |

oon ah'bee-toh kom-play'toh.

| Coat, trousers, waistcoat. | Giacca, pantaloni, panciotto. |

jahk'kah, pahn-tah-loh'nee, pahn-chot'toh.

| A dress, a blouse, a skirt. | Un vestito, una camicetta (blusa), una sottana. |

oon vess-tee'toh, oo'nah kah-mee-chet'tah (bloo'zah), oo'nah sot-tah'nah.

Cardigan, pullover, twin set. | Golf, pullover, completo (di maglia) a due pezzi.

golf, (as in English), kom-play'toh (dee mahl'yah) ah doo'ay pet'see.

An overcoat, a mackintosh. | Un soprabito (càpotto, mantello), un impermeabile.

oon soh-prah'bee-toh (kah-pot'toh, mahn-tell'loh), oon im-pehr-may-ah'bee-lay.

A pair of gloves. | Un paio di guanti.

oon pah'yoh dee gwahn'tee.

A tie, a shawl, scarf. | Una cravatta, uno scialle, una sciarpa.

oo'nah krah-vaht'tah, oo'noh shahl'lay, oo'nah shahr'pah.

The boot shop. | Il calzolaio.

eel kahlt-soh-lah'yoh.

Shoes, boots. | Scarpe (basse), scarpe (alte).

skahr'pay (bahs'say), (ahl'tay).

Slippers, goloshes. | Pantofole, soprascarpe.

pahn-toh'foh-lay, soh-prah-skahr'pay.

A pair of laces, boot polish. | Un paio di stringhe (lacci), vernice.

oon pah'yoh dee streeng'gay (lahch'chee), vehr-nee'chay.

The hat shop. | Il cappellaio, la modista.

eel kahp-pell-lah'yoh, lah moh-dee'stah.

A soft hat, a cap. | Un cappello floscio, un berretto.

oon kahp-pell'loh flosh'shoh, oon behr-ret'toh.

My size is ——. | La mia misura è ——.

lah mee'ah mee-zoo'rah ay . . .

The size of hats and collars is measured in centimetres, but in good quality collars the English measurement is marked as well. Shoes are measured on a different system (the numbers for children's shoes go from 16 to 38, for women's from 34 to 42, and for men's from 39 to 46).

May I try it ? | Posso provarlo ?

poss'soh proh-vahr'loh ?

| I should like to try on the —— I saw in the window. | Vorrei provare —— che ho visto in vetrina. |

vor-ray'ee proh-vah'ray . . . kay oh vee'stoh in vay-tree'nah.

| This is too narrow (wide). | Questo è troppo stretto (largo). |

kwess'toh ay trop'poh stret'toh (lahr'goh).

| I don't like this. | Questo non mi piace. |

kwess'toh non mee pee-ah'chay.

| I don't like the colour. | Non mi piace il colore. |

non mee pee-ah'chay eel koh-lor'ray.

| Please show me ——. | Per favore, mi fa vedere ——. |

pehr fah-vor'ray mee fah vay-day'ray . . .

| Have you anything better (cheaper)? | Non ha qualcosa di meglio (di meno caro)? |

non ah kwahl-koh'zah dee mayl'yoh (dee may'noh kah'roh)?

| I will take it with me. | Lo prendo con me. |

loh pren'doh kon may.

| Please send it. | Me lo mandi, per favore. |

may loh mahn'dee, pehr fah-vor'ray.

| My address is ——. | Il mio indirizzo è ——. |

eel mee'oh in-dee-reet'soh ay . . .

| I will pay on delivery. | Pagherò alla consegna. |

pah-gay-roh' ahl'lah kon-sayn'yah.

FOOD

See also " Meals," the Menu, page 85.

| The fruiterer. | Il fruttivendolo, l'ortolano. |

eel froot-tee-ven'doh-loh, lorr-toh-lah'noh.

| Some fruit. | Della frutta. |

dell'lah froot'tah.

| Apples, apricots, bananas. | Mele, albicocche, banane. |

may'lay, ahl-bee-kock'kay, bah-nah'nay.

| Grapes, lemons, oranges, melon. | Uva, limoni, arance, melone (popone). |

oo'vah, lee-moh'nee, ah-rahn'chay, may-loh'nay (poh-poh'nay).

| Peaches, pears, plums. | Pesche, pere, prugne (susine). |

pess'kay, pay'ray, proon'yay (soo-zee'nay).

| Pineapple, strawberries, walnuts. | Ananas, fragole, noci. |

ah-nah-nahss', frah'goh-lay, noh'chee.

| How much a kilo ? | Quanto al chilo ? |

kwahn'toh ahl kee'loh ?

| The baker. | Il fornaio. |

eel forr-nah'yoh.

| Some bread, rolls. | Del pane, panini. |

dell pah'nay, pah-nee'nee.

| The pastrycook, cake shop. | Il pasticcere, pasticceria. |

eel pah-steech-chay'ray, pah-steech-chay-ree'ah.

| Chocolate, chocolates. | Cioccolato, cioccolatini. |

chock-koh-lah'toh, chock-koh-lah-tee'nee.

| Cakes, sweets. | Dolci, caramelle. |

doll'chee, kah-rah-mell'lay.

| The butcher. | Il macellaio. |

eel mah-chell-lah'yoh.

| The fishmonger. | Il pescivendolo. |

eel pay-shee-ven'doh-loh.

| The milkman. | Il lattaio. |

eel laht-tah'yoh.

| The grocer. | Il droghiere, pizzicagnolo. |

eel droh-ghee-ay'ray, peet-see-kahn'yoh-loh.

REPAIRS

| This doesn't work. | Questo non funziona. |

kwess'toh non foont-see-oh'nah.

| Can you repair this ? | Può riparare (accomodare) questo ? |

poo-oh' ree-pah-rah'ray (ahk-koh-moh-dah'ray) kwess'toh ?

| I have broken ——. | Ho rotto ——. |
| | oh rot'toh . . . |

| I have torn ——. | Ho strappato ——. |
| | oh strahp-pah'toh . . . |

| Can you patch this tear ? | Può accomodare questo strappo ? |

poo-oh' ahk-koh-moh-dah'ray kwess'toh strahp'poh ?

| Can you darn (stitch) this ? | Può rammendare (cucire) questo ? |

poo-oh' rahm-men-dah'ray (koo-chee'ray) kwess'toh ?

| This stocking is laddered. | Questa calza è sfilata. |

kwess'tah kahlt'sah ay sfee-lah'tah.

| How much will that cost ? | Quanto costerà ? |

kwahn'toh koss-tay-rah' ?

| How long will that take ? | Quanto tempo ci vorrà ? |

kwahn'toh tem'poh chee vor-rah' ?

| I can leave it for two days only. | Posso lasciarlo per due giorni soli. |

poss'soh lah-shahr'loh pehr doo'ay jorr'nee soh'lee.

| My watch wants cleaning. | Il mio orologio ha bisogno di essere ripulito. |

eel mee'oh oh-roh-loh'joh ah bee-zohn'yoh dee ess'say-ray roo poo lee'toh.

| My watch has stopped. | Il mio orologio si è fermato. |

eel mee'oh oh-roh-loh'joh see ay fehr-mah'toh.

| Please regulate it. | Favorisca regolarlo. |

fah-voh-ree'skah ray-goh-lahr'loh.

| The lock is broken. | La serratura è rotta. |

lah sehr-rah-too'rah ay rot'tah.

| I have lost the key. | Ho perso la chiave. |

oh pehr'soh lah kee-ah'vay.

| Spectacles, the lens. | Occhiali, la lente. |

ock-kee-ah'lee, lah len'tay.

| I want these shoes soled. | Vorrei far risuolare queste scarpe. |

vor-ray'ee fahr ree-soo-oh-lah'ray kwess'tay skahr'pay.

Will you put some nails in these boots ?	Vuol mettere dei chiodi a queste scarpe ?

voo-ohl′ met′tay-ray day′ee kee-oh′ dee ah kwess′tay skahr′pay ?

Can you repair the heels?	Può rifare i tacchi ?

poo-oh′ ree-fah′ray ee tahk′kee ?

Where is the cleaner's ?	Dov'è la tintoria ?

doh-vay′ lah teen-toh-ree′ah ?

Can you clean (dry-clean) this dress (this coat) ?	Può pulire (pulire a secco) questo vestito (questo capotto) ?

poo-oh′ poo-lee′ray (poo-lee′ray ah seck′koh) kwess′toh vess-tee′toh (kwess′toh kah-pot′toh) ?

How soon will it be ready ?	Per quando sarà fatto ?

pehr kwahn′doh sah-rah′ faht′toh ?

GENERAL SHOPPING VOCABULARY

See also " Clothing," page 74, " Food," page 77, and " Sundry Articles," page 82.

Alarm clock.	Sveglia.

svayl′yah.

Belt, brooch.	Cintura, spilla.

chin-too′rah, spill′lah.

Brush, comb.	Spazzola, pettine.

spaht′soh-lah, pet′tee-nay.

Cream (face).	Crema per il viso.

kray′mah pehr eel vee′zoh.

Field glasses, opera glasses.	Binocolo, binocolo da teatro.

bee-noh′koh-loh, bee-noh′koh-loh dah tay-ah′troh.

Gramophone records.	Dischi per grammofono.

diss′kee pehr grahm-moh′fah-noh.

Hair brush, hairpins.	Spazzola per capelli, forcine.

spaht′soh-lah pehr kah-pell′lee, forr-chee′nay.

Hand-bag (ladies'), wallet. | Borsa per signora, portafogli.

borr'sah pehr seen-yor'rah, porr-tah-foll'yee.

Lipstick, rouge, mirror. | Rosso per le labbra, rossetto, specchio.

ross'soh pehr lay lahb'brah, ross-set'toh, speck'kee-oh.

Parasol. | Ombrellino.

om-brell-lee'noh.

Powder (face), purse. | Cipria, portamonete.

chee'pree-ah, porr-tah-moh-nay'tay.

Razor, safety razor. | Rasoio, rasoio di sicurezza.

rah-zoh'yoh, rah-zoh'yoh dee see-koo-ret'sah.

Razor blades. | Lame per rasoio.

lah'may pehr rah-zoh'yoh.

Ring. | Anello.

ah-nell'loh.

Shaving brush, (shaving) soap. | Pennello per barba, sapone (per barba).

pen-nell'loh pehr bahr'bah, sah-poh'nay (pehr bahr'bah).

Stick, suit case. | Bastone, valigia.

bah-stoh'nay, vah-lee'jah.

Sun-glasses. | Occhiali per il sole.

ock-kee-ah'lee pehr eel soh'lay.

Tooth-brush, -paste. | Spazzolino da denti, pasta dentifricia.

spaht-soh-lee'noh dah den'tee, pah'stah den-tee-free'chah.

Towel, trunk. | Asciugamano, baule.

ah-shoo-gah-mah'noh, bah-oo'lay.

Umbrella, watch. | Ombrello, orologio.

om-brell'loh, oh-roh-loh'joh.

Of gold, silver. | D'oro, d'argento.

dor'roh, dahr-jen'toh.

For gentlemen (for ladies). | Per uomo (per signora).

pehr oo-oh'moh (pehr seen-yor'rah).

DIFFICULTIES

You have not given me the right change.	Lei ha sbagliato nel darmi il resto.

lay'ee ah sbahl-yah'toh nell dahr'mee eel ress'toh.

I bought this in your shop.	Ho comprato questo nel suo negozio.

oh kom-prah'toh kwess'toh nell soo'oh nay-got'see-oh.

It does not work ; it does not fit me.	Non funziona ; non mi va.

non funt-see-oh'nah ; non mee vah.

Can you change it ?	Me lo può cambiare ?

may loh poo-oh'kahm-bee-ah'ray ?

Can you return me the money ?	Mi può restituire il denaro ?

mee poo-oh' ress-tee-too-ee'ray eel day-nah'roh ?

SUNDRY ARTICLES

A list of articles likely to be required at short notice.

String, rope.	Uno spago, una corda.

oo'noh spah'goh, oo'nah korr'dah.

A strap.	Una cinghia.

oo'nah cheeng'ghee-ah.

Some thread, scissors.	Del filo, un paio di forbici.

dell fee'loh, oon pah'yoh dee forr'bee-chee.

Buttons, hooks and eyes, press studs, zip-fastening, tape.	Bottoni, ganci e magliette, automatici, chiusura lampo, nastro d'Olanda.

bot-toh'nee, gahn'chee ay mahl-yet'tay, ow-toh-mah'tee-chee, kee-oo-zoo'rah lahm'poh, nah'stroh doh-lahn'dah.

A (safety) pin, a needle.	Uno spillo (di sicurezza), un ago.

oo'noh spill'loh (dee see-koo-ret'sah), oon ah'goh.

A small (big) box.	Una scatola piccola (grande).

oo'nah skah'toh-lah peek'koh-lah (grahn'day).

(Wrapping), (tissue) paper. | Carta (da imballaggio), (velina).

kahr'tah (dah im-bahl-lahd'joh), (vay-lee'nah).

COLOURS

Blue, black, brown. | Blu, nero, marrone.

bloo, nay'roh, mahr-roh'nay.

Green, grey. | Verde, grigio.

vehr'day, gree'joh.

Orange, pink, red. | Arancione, rosa, rosso.

ah-rahn-choh'nay, roh'zah, ross'soh.

Violet, white, yellow. | Viola, bianco, giallo.

vee-oh'lah, bee-ahng'koh, jahl'loh.

Light ——, dark ——. | —— chiaro, ——scuro.

—— kee-ah' roh, —— skoo'roh.

I want a lighter (darker) shade. | Vorrei una tinta più chiara (più scura).

vor-ray'ee oo'nah teen'tah pee-oo' kee-ah'rah (pee-oo'skoo'rah).

MEALS [1]

FINDING A RESTAURANT AND TABLE

Where is there a good restaurant ? | Dove c'è un buon ristorante ?

doh'vay chay oon boo-ohn' ree-stoh-rahn'tay ?

Can we dine here ? | Si può pranzare qui ?

see poo-oh' prahnt-sah'ray kwee ?

Can we dine at once ? | Si può pranzare subito ?

see poo-oh' prahnt-sah'ray soo'bee-toh ?

Where can I have a wash ? | Dove mi posso lavare ?

doh'vay mee poss'soh lah-vah'ray ?

Will you keep a table for three (four) ? | Vuol tenere (riservare) una tavola per tre (quattro) persone ?

voo-ohl' tay-nay'ray (ree-zehr-vah'ray) oo'nah tah'voh-lah pehr tray (kwaht'troh) pehr-soh'nay ?

[1] See Introduction, page 12.

| Is this table free ? | È libera questa tavola ? |
| | ay lee′bay-rah kwess′tah tah′voh-lah ? |

| Give me a table near the window. | Mi dia una tavola vicino alla finestra. |

mee dee′ah oo′nah tah′voh-lah vee-chee′noh ahl′lah fee-ness′trah.

| In the corner. | Nell'angolo. |
| | nell lahng′goh-loh. |

| Is there a table d'hôte ? | C'è un pranzo a prezzo fisso ? |

chay oon prahnt′soh ah pret′soh fiss′soh ?

| I will order à la carte. | Vorrei pranzare alla carta. |
| | vor-ray′ee prahnt-sah′ray ahl′lah kahr′tah. |

| Please serve me (us) quickly. | Per favore, mi (ci) serva in fretta. |

pehr fah-vor′ray, mee (chee) sehr′vah in fret′tah.

DURING THE MEAL

| Bring me the bill of fare. | Mi porti la lista. |
| | mee porr′tee lah lee′stah. |

| The wine list. | La carta dei vini. |
| | lah kahr′tah day′ee vee′nee. |

| Is there a good wine of the neighbourhood ? | C'è un buon vino del posto ? |

chay oon boo-ohn′ vee′noh dell poss′toh ?

| Waiter ! | Cameriere ! |
| | kah-may-ree-ay′ray ! |

| The plates are cold. | I piatti sono freddi. |
| | ee pee-aht′tee soh′noh fred′dee. |

| This is not clean. | Questo non è pulito. |
| | kwess′toh non ay poo-lee′toh. |

| This is not properly cooked. | Questo non è cucinato bene. |

kwess′toh non ay koo-chee-nah′toh bay′nay.

| I like it underdone (well done). | Lo desidero poco cotto (ben cotto). |

loh day-zee′day-roh poh′koh kot′toh (benn kot′toh).

This is not fresh.	Questo non è fresco.
kwess'toh non ay fress'koh.	
Some more bread, please.	Mi dia dell'altro pane.
mee dee'ah dell-lahl'troh pah'nay.	
This piece is too fat.	Questo pezzo è troppo grasso.
kwess'toh pet'soh ay trop'poh grahs'soh.	
I don't like this.	Non mi piace questo.
non mee pee-ah'chay kwess'toh.	
I prefer the leg, wing, breast.	Preferisco la coscia, l'ala, il petto.
pray-fay-ree'skoh lah koh'shah, lah'lah, eel pet'toh.	
Bring me another helping.	Mi porti un'altra porzione.
mee porr'tee oon-ahl'trah port-see-oh'nay.	
I have had enough.	Ne ho preso abbastanza.
nay oh pray'zoh ahb-bah-stahnt'sah.	
No, thank you.	No, grazie.
no(r), graht'see-ay.	
Yes, please.	Sì, per piacere.
see, pehr pee-ah-chay'ray.	

VOCABULARY OF MENU

Artichokes, asparagus.	Carciofi, asparagi.
kahr-choh'fee, ah-spah'rah-jee.	
Beans (French).	Fagiolini.
fah-joh-lee'nee.	
Beans (broad).	Fagioli.
fah-joh'lee.	
Beef, boiled.	Manzo lesso.
mahnd'zoh less'soh.	
Beef, roast.	Manzo arrosto.
mahnd'zoh ahr-ross'toh.	
Beer, biscuits.	Birra, biscotti.
beer'rah, bee-skot'tee.	
Boiled, grilled, roast.	Lesso, alla griglia, arrosto.
less'soh, ahl'lah greel'yah, ahr-ross'toh.	

Brandy, broth. | Cognac, brodo.
kohn-yahk', broh'doh.

Bread, butter. | Pane, burro.
pah'nay, boor'roh.

Cabbage. | Cavolo.
kah'voh-loh.

Carrots, cauliflower. | Carote, cavolfiore.
kah-roh'tay, kah-voll-fee-or'ray.

Caviar, celery. | Caviale, sedano.
kah-vee-ah'lay, say'dah-noh.

Cheese, chicken. | Formaggio, pollo.
forr-mahd'joh, poll'loh.

Cod. | Merluzzo.
mehr-loot'soh.

Coffee (with milk). | Caffè (latte).
kahf-fay' (laht'tay).

Cold meat. | Carne fredda.
kahr'nay fred'dah.

Cucumber. | Cetriolo.
chay-tree-oh'loh.

Cutlet (veal). | Costoletta (di vitello).
koss-toh-let'tah (dee vee-tell'loh).

Dessert, dinner. | Dessert, pranzo.
dess-sehr', prahnt'soh.

Duck. | Anitra.
ah'nee-trah.

Eggs, boiled. | Uova à la coque.
oo-oh'vah ah lah kock.

Eggs, fried, poached. | Uova al tegame, affogate.
oo-oh'vah ahl tay-gah'may, ahf-foh-gah'tay.

Fish, fried, boiled. | Pesce fritto, in bianco.
pay'shay fritt'toh, in bee-ahng'koh.

Game, goose, hare. | Selvaggina, oca, lepre.
sell-vahd-jee'nah, oh'kah, lay'pray.

Ham, herrings. | Prosciutto, aringhe.
proh-shoot'toh, ah-reeng'gay.

Hors d'œuvre. | Antipasto.
ahn-tee-pah'stoh.

Ice, ice-cream. | Ghiaccio, gelato.

ghee-ahch'choh, jay-lah'toh.

Italian champagne. | Spumante.

spoo-mahn'tay.

Jam. | Marmellata.

mahr-mell-lah'tah.

Kid, kidney. | Capretto, rognone.

kah-prett'toh, rohn-yoh'nay.

Lamb. | Agnello.

ahn-yell'loh.

Lemon, lemonade. | Limone, limonata
| (spremuta di limone).

lee-moh'nay, lee-moh-nah'tah (spray-moo'tah dee lee-moh'nay).

Lettuce, liver. | Lattuga, fegato.

laht-too'gah, fay'gah-toh.

Liqueurs. | Liquori.

lee-kwor'ree.

Lobster, lunch. | Aragosta, colazione.

ah-rah-goss'tah, koh-laht-see-oh'nay.

Macaroni (with butter and cheese; with gravy; with tomato sauce). | Pasta asciutta (in bianco; al sugo : alla salsa di pomodoro).

pah'stah ah-shoot'tah (in bee-ahng'koh; ahl soo'goh; ahl'lah sahl'sah dee poh-moh-dor'roh).

Mackerel. | Sgombro.

zgom'broh.

Milk, mineral water. | Latte, acqua minerale.

laht'tay, ahk'kwah mee-nay-rah'lay.

Mushrooms, mustard. | Funghi, senape.

foong'ghee, say'nah-pay.

Oil, olives. | Olio, olive.

oll'yoh, oh-lee'vay.

Omelette, onions. | Frittata (omelette),
| cipolle.

fritt-tah'tah (omm-lett'), chee-poll'lay.

Oysters, partridge. | Ostriche, pernice.

oss'tree-kay, pehr-nee'chay.

Pastry, small cakes.	Pasticceria.
	pah-steech-chay-ree'ah.
Peas.	Piselli.
	pee-zell'lee.
Pepper, pickles.	Pepe, sott'aceti.
	pay'pay, sot-tah-chay'tee.
Pheasant.	Fagiano.
	fah-jah'noh.
Port (wine).	(Vino di) Oporto.
	(vee'noh dee) oh-porr'toh.
Pork.	Maiale.
	mah-yah'lay.
Potatoes (fried).	Patate (fritte).
	pah-tah'tay (frit'tay).
Potatoes, mashed.	Puré di patate.
	poo-ray' dee pah-tah'tay.
Pudding.	Dolce.
	doll'chay.
Red mullet.	Triglia.
	treel'yah.
Rabbit, ragout.	Coniglio, ragù.
	koh-neel'yoh, rah-goo.
Rice soup (clear).	Riso in brodo.
	ree'zoh in broh'doh.
Rice (with butter or gravy).	Risotto.
	ree-zot'toh.
Salad, salt.	Insalata, sale.
	in-sah-lah'tah, sah'lay.
Salmon, sardines.	Salmone, sardine.
	sahl-moh'nay, sahr-dee'nay.
Sandwich, sausage.	Panino imbottito, tartina ; salsiccia, salame.
pah-nee'noh im-bot-tee'toh, tahr-tee'nah, sahl-seech'chah, sah-lah'may.	
Soda water.	Acqua di seltz.
	ahk'kwah dee selts.
Sole.	Sogliola.
	soll'yoh-lah.

Soup, clear.	Consommé, minestrina.

kon-som-may′, mee-ness-tree′nah.

Soup, thick.	Crema, minestrone.

kray′mah, mee-ness-troh′nay.

Spinach, steak.	Spinaci, bistecca.

spee-nah′chee, bee-steck′kah.

Stewed fruit.	Composta di frutta, frutta cotta.

kom-poss′tah dee froot′tah, froot′tah kot′tah.

Sugar.	Zucchero.

zook′kay-roh.

Supper, tea.	Cena, thè.

chay′nah, tay.

Toast.	Pane tostato, crostini.

pan′ray toss-tah′toh, kross-tee′nee.

Tomatoes, tomato sauce.	Pomodori, salsa di pomodoro.

poh-moh-dor′ree, sahl′sah dee poh-moh-dor′roh.

Tongue, trout.	Lingua, trota.

leeng′gwah, troh′tah.

Truffles, turbot.	Tartufi, rombo.

tahr-too′fee, rom′boh.

Turnip, turkey.	Rapa, tacchino.

rah′pah, tahk-kee′noh.

Veal.	Vitello.

vee-tell′loh.

Vegetables.	Legumi, verdura.

lay-goo′mee, vehr-doo′rah.

Vinegar.	Aceto.

ah-chay′toh.

Water.	Acqua.

ahk′kwah.

Whiting.	Nasello.

nah-zell′loh.

Wine.	Vino.

vee′noh.

Red (white) wine.	Vino rosso (bianco).

vee′noh ross′soh (bee-ahng′koh).

UTENSILS

Bottle, cup, jug. | Bottiglia, tazza, brocca.
bot-teel'yah, taht'sah, brock'kah.

Fork, glass. | Forchetta, bicchiere.
forr-ket'tah, bick-kee-ay'ray.

Knife, a sharp knife. | Coltello, un coltello
                                   affilato.
koll-tell'loh, oon koll tell'loh ahf-fee-lah'toh.

Napkin, plate. | Tovagliolo, piatto.
toh-vahl-yoh'loh, pee-aht'toh.

Spoon, (dessert, table). | Cucchiaio.
kook-kee-ah'yoh.

Spoon, tea. | Cucchiaino.
kook-kee-ah-ee'noh.

Table-cloth. | Tovaglia.
toh-vahl'yah.

Tea-pot, toothpick. | Teiera, stecchino.
tay-ee-ay'rah, steck-kee'noh.

PAYING THE BILL

The bill, please. | Il conto, per favore.
eel kon'toh, pehr fah-vor'ray.

Is the service included ? | E' compreso il servizio ?
ay kom-pray'zoh eel sehr-veet'see-oh ?

Keep the change for | Tenga il resto per sè.
   yourself. |
teng'gah eel ress'toh pehr say.

DIFFICULTIES

There is a mistake in | C'è un errore nel conto.
   the bill. |
chay oon ehr-ror'ray nell kon'toh.

Check it, please. | Lo verifichi, per favore.
loh vay-ree'fee-kee, pehr fah-vor'ray.

What is this for ? | Questo che cosa è ?
kwess'toh kay koh'zah ay ?

I did not have ——. | Non ho preso ——.
non oh pray'zoh . . .

| I only had ——. | Ho avuto soltanto ——. |

oh ah-voo′toh soll-tahn′toh . .

| Ask the head waiter to come here. | Dica al capo servizio di venire qui. |

dee′kah ahl kah′poh sehr-veet′see-oh dee vay-nee′ray
kwee.

ACCIDENT AND ILLNESS

ACCIDENT

| Send for a policeman (an ambulance). | Chiami una guardia (un'ambulanza). |

kee-ah′mee oo′nah gwahr′dee-ah (oon ahm-boo-lahnt′sah).

| There has been an accident. | C'è stata una disgrazia. |

chay stah′tah oo′nah dees-graht′see-ah.

| Someone has fallen in the water. | Qualcuno è caduto nell'acqua. |

kwahl-koo′noh ay kah-doo′toh nell lahk′kwah.

| Bring some cold water, some brandy. | Porti dell'acqua fredda, del cognac. |

porr′tee dell lahk′kwah fred′dah, dell kohn-yahk′.

| Have you any bandages ? | Ha delle bende ? |

ah dell lay ben′day ?

| Are you hurt ? | Si è fatto male ? |

see ay faht′toh mah′lay ?

| Are you feeling better ? | Si sente meglio ? |

see sen′tay mayl′yoh ?

| He (she) is seriously injured. | E' ferito (ferita) gravemente. |

ay fay-ree′toh (fay-ree′tah) grah-vay-men′tav.

| Is there a doctor (a chemist) near here ? | C'è un dottore (una farmacia) qui vicino ? |

chay oon dot-tor′ray (oo′nah fahr-mah-chee′ah) kwee
vee-chee′noh ?

| It hurts me here. | Mi fa male qui. |

mee fah mah′lay kwee.

I can't move. | Non mi posso muovere.
non mee poss'soh moo-oh'vay-ray.

I have broken (dislocated) my ——. | Mi sono rotto (slogato). ——.
mee soh'noh rot'toh (sloh-gah'toh) . . .

I have cut my ——. | Mi sono tagliato ——.
mee soh'noh tahl-yah'toh . . .

Ankle, arm. | Caviglia, braccio.
kah-veel'yah, brahch'choh.

Back, bone, elbow. | Schiena, osso, gomito.
skee-ay'nah, oss'soh, goh'mee-toh.

Face, finger, foot. | Faccia, dito, piede.
fahch'chah, dee'toh, pee-ay'day.

Hand, head, hip, knee. | Mano, testa, anca, ginocchio.
mah'noh, tess'tah, ahng'kah, jee-nock'kee-oh.

Leg, neck, nose. | Gamba, collo, naso.
gahm'bah, koll'loh, nah'zoh.

Shoulder, wrist. | Spalla, polso.
spahl'lah, poll'soh.

He (she) has fainted. | E' svenuto (svenuta).
ay svay-noo'toh (svay-noo'tah).

Help me to carry him (her). | Mi aiuti a trasportarlo (trasportarla).
mee ah-yoo'tee ah trah-sporr-tahr'loh (trah-sporr-tahr'lah).

It is swollen. | Sì è gonfiato.
see ay gon-fee-ah'toh.

It is bleeding. | Sanguina.
sahng'gwee-nah.

Can you dress this wound ? | Può medicare (fasciare) questa ferita ?
poo-oh' may-dee-kah'ray (fah-shah'ray) kwess'tah fay-ree'tah ?

AT THE DOCTOR'S
See also " The Chemist," page 70.

I have pains in ——.	Ho male a ——, mi fa male —— (sing.), mi fanno male — (plur.).

oh mah'lay ah . . . mee fah mah'lay . . . mee fahn'noh mah'lay.

The back, the chest.	La schiena, il petto.

lah skee-ay'nah, eel pet'toh.

The ear, the head.	L'orecchio, la testa.

lor-reck'kee-oh, lah tess'tah.

The eyes, the heart.	Gli occhi, il cuore.

lyee ock'kee, eel kwor'ray.

The joints, the kidneys, the intestine.	Le giunture, i reni, l'intestino.

lay joon-too'ray, ee ray'nee, lin-tess-tee'noh

The liver, the lungs.	Il fegato, i polmoni.

eel fay'gah-toh, ee poll-moh'nee.

The stomach, the throat, the tongue.	Lo stomaco, la gola, la lingua.

loh stoh'mah-koh, lah goh'lah, lah leeng'gwah.

Cramp, fever, fit.	Crampo, febbre, accesso (attacco).

krahm'poh, feb'bray, ahch-chess'soh (aht-tahk'koh).

I am shivering.	Ho dei brividi.

oh day'ee bree'vee-dee.

I have a temperature.	Ho la febbre.

oh lah feb'bray.

Indigestion, nausea.	Indigestione, nausea.

in-dee-jess-tee-oh'nay, now'zay-ah.

Poisoning.	Avvelenamento, intossicazione.

ahv-vay-lay-lay-nah-men'toh, in-toss-see-kaht-see-oh'nay.

Rheumatism, vomit.	Reumatismo, vomito.

ray-oo-mah-tees'moh, voh'mee-toh.

The medicine, the remedy.	La medicina, il rimedio.

lah may-dee-chee'nah, eel ree-may'dee-oh.

| I am not sleeping well. | Dormo male. |

dorr'moh mah'lay.

| I cannot eat. | Non posso mangiare. |

non poss'soh mahn-jah'ray.

| I have no appetite. | Non ho appetito. |

non oh ahp-pay-tee'toh.

| Must I stay in bed? | Devo stare a letto? |

day'voh stah'ray ah let'toh?

| When will you come? | Quando ritornerà? |

kwahn'doh ree-torr-nay-rah'?

| I feel better. | Mi sento meglio. |

mee sen'toh mayl'yoh.

When do you think I	Quando crede che mi
shall be fit to travel?	potrò mettere in
	viaggio?

kwahn'doh kray'day kay mee poh-troh' met'tay-ray in vee-ahd'joh?

| What is your fee? | Quanto Le devo? |

kwahn'toh lay day'voh?

AT THE DENTIST'S

| Can you recommend me | Mi può indicare un buon |
| a good dentist? | dentista? |

mee poo-oh' in-dee-kah'ray oon boo-ohn' den-tee'stah.

| I want to make an | Vorrei fissare un |
| appointment. | appuntamento. |

vor-ray'ee fiss-sah'ray oon ahp-poon-tah-men'toh.

| I have toothache. | Ho mal di denti. |

oh mahl dee den'tee.

| This tooth aches. | Questo dente mi fa male. |

kwess'toh den'tay mee fah mah'lay.

| The gums are sore. | Le gengive mi fanno male. |

lay jen-jee'vay mee fahn'noh mah'lay.

| I have an abscess. | Ho un ascesso. |

oh oon ah-shess'soh.

| Can it be stopped? | Si può otturare? |

see poo-oh' ot-too-rah'ray?

Is it necessary to take it out ?	Bisogna estrarlo ?

bee-zohn′yah ess-trahr′loh ?

It is very painful.	Fa molto male.

fah moll′toh mah′lay.

Filling.	Otturazione (piombatura).

ot-too-raht-see-oh′nay, pee-om-bah-too′rah.

Denture, false teeth.	Dentiera.

den-tee-ay′rah.

Gold crown.	Corona d'oro.

koh-roh′nah dor′roh.

Am I to come again ?	Devo ritornare ?

day′voh ree-torr-nah′ray ?

I am leaving here on the —.	Parto il ——.

pahr′toh eel ——.

COUNTRIES, TOWNS AND NATIONALITIES

The word " Inghilterra " (England) is commonly used in Italy to mean Great Britain or the British Isles.

America, American.	America, americano.[1]

ah-may ree-kah, ah-may-ree-kah′noh.

North, South America.	America del Nord, del Sud.

ah-may′ree-kah dell norrd, dell sood.

Austria, Austrian.	Austria, austriaco.

ow′stree-ah, ow-stree′ah-koh.

Belgium, Belgian.	Belgio, belga.

bell′joh, bell′gah.

Czechoslovakia, Czechoslovakian.	Ceco-slovacchia, ceco(slovacco).

chay-koh-sloh-vahk-kee′ah, chay′koh (-sloh-vahk′koh).

[1] *Nouns and adjectives denoting nationality are written with small letters in Italian.*

Denmark, Danish, Dane. | Danimarca, danese.
dah-nee-mahr'kah, dah-nay'zay.

Egypt, Egyptian. | Egitto, egiziano.
ay-jeet'toh, ay-jeet-see-ah'noh.

England, English, Englishman. | Inghilterra, inglese.
eeng-gheel-tehr'rah, eeng-glay'zay.

France, French, Frenchman. | Francia, francese.
frahn chah, frahn-chay'zay.

Germany, German. | Germania, tedesco.
jehr-mah'nee-ah, tay-dess'koh.

Great Britain, British. | Gran Bretagna (Inghilterra), britannico (inglese).
grahn bray-tahn'yah (eeng-gheel-tehr'rah), bree-tahn'nee-koh (eeng-glay'zay).

Holland, Dutch, Dutchman. | Olanda, olandese.
oh-lahn'dah, oh-lahn-day'zay.

Hungary, Hungarian. | Ungheria, ungherese.
oong-gay-ree'ah, oong-gay-ray'zay.

Ireland, Irish, Irishman. | Irlanda, irlandese.
eer-lahn'dah, eer-lahn-day'zay.

Italy, Italian. | Italia, italiano.
ee-tah'lee-ah, ee-tah-lee-ah'noh.

Norway, Norwegian. | Norvegia, norvegese.
norr-vay'jah, norr-vay-jay'zay.

Poland, Pole, Polish. | Polonia, polacco.
poh-loh'nee-ah, poh-lahk'koh.

Russia, Russian. | Russia, russo.
roos'see-ah, roos'soh.

Scotland, Scottish, Scotsman. | Scozia, scozzese.
skot'see-ah, skot-say'zay.

Spain, Spanish, Spaniard. | Spagna, spagnolo.
spahn'yah, spahn-yoh'loh.

Sweden, Swedish, Swede. | Svezia, svedese.

svayt'see-ah, svay-day'zay.

Switzerland, Swiss. | Svizzera, svizzero.

sveet'say-rah, sveet-say'roh.

Turkey, Turkish, Turk. | Turchia, turco.

toor-kee'ah, toor'koh.

United States. | Stati Uniti.

stah'tee oo-nee'tee.

Yugoslavia, Yugoslav. | Jugoslavia, jugoslavo.

yoo-goh-slah'vee-ah, yoo-goh-slah'voh.

London, Paris, Geneva. | Londra, Parigi,

Ginevra.

lonn'drah, pah-ree'jee, jee-nay'vrah.

Bâle, Cologne, Munich. | Basilea, Colonia,

Monaco.

bah-zee-lay'ah, koh-loh'nee-ah, moh'nah-koh.

Lausanne, Berne. | Losanna, Berna.

loh-zahn'nah, behr'nah.

Lyons, Marseilles, Nice. | Lione, Marsiglia, Nizza.

lee-oh'nay, mahr-seel'yah, neet'sah.

Turin, Milan, Venice. | Torino, Milano,

Venezia.

toh-ree'noh, mee-lah'noh, vay-net'see-ah.

Genoa, Florence, | Genova, Firenze,

Leghorn. | Livorno.

jay'noh-vah, fee-rent'say, lee-vorr'noh.

Rome, Naples, Sardinia, | Roma, Napoli, Sardegna,

Sicily. | Sicilia.

roh'mah, nah'poh-lee, sahr-dayn'yah, see-chee'lee-ah.

English Channel. | La Manica.

lah mah'nee-kah.

Mediterranean Sea. | Mediterraneo.

may-dee-tehr-rah'nay-oh.

The Atlantic, the Pacific. | L'Atlantico, il Pacifico.

laht-lahn'tee-koh, eel pah-chee'fee-koh.

North Sea, Baltic Sea. | Mare del Nord, Mar

Baltico.

mah'ray dell norrd, mahr bahl'tee-koh.

The Italian Lakes. | I Laghi italiani.
ee lah′ghee ee-tah-lee-ah′nee.
Tyrrhenian, Adriatic Sea. | Mar Tirreno, Adriatico.
mahr teer-ray′noh, ah-dree-ah′tee-koh.

NUMBERS

1 Uno, una.
oo′noh, oo′nah.

2 Due.
doo′ay.

3 Tre.
tray.

4 Quattro.
kwaht′troh.

5 Cinque.
cheeng′kway.

6 Sei.
say′ee.

7 Sette.
set′tay.

8 Otto.
ot′toh.

9 Nove.
noh′vay.

10 Dieci.
dee-ay′chee.

11 Undici.
oon′dee-chee.

12 Dodici.
doh′dee-chee.

13 Tredici.
tray′dee-chee.

14 Quattordici.
kwaht-torr′dee-chee.

15 Quindici.
kween′dee-chee.

16 Sedici.
say′dee-chee.

17 Diciassette.
dee-chahs-set′tay.

18 Diciotto.
dee-chot′toh.

19 Diciannove.
dee-chahn-noh′vay.

20 Venti.
ven′tee.

21 Ventuno.
ven-too′noh.

22 Ventidue.
ven-tee-doo′ay.

28 Ventotto.
ven-t. t′toh.

30 Trenta.
tren′tah.

40 Quaranta.
kwah-rahn′tah.

50 Cinquanta.
cheeng-kwahn′tah.

60 Sessanta.
sess-sahn′tah.

70 Settanta.
set-tahn′tah.

80 Ottanta.
ot-tahn′tah.

90 Novanta.
noh-vahn′tah.

100 Cento. chen'toh.	2,000 Duemila. doo-ay-mee'lah.
200 Duecento. doo-ay-chen'toh.	100,000 Centomila. chen-toh-mee'lah.
1,000 Mille. mill'lay.	A million Un milione. oon mee-lee-oh'nay.
First Primo. pree'moh.	Ninth Nono. noh'noh.
Second Secondo. say-kon'doh.	Tenth Decimo. day'chee-moh.
Third Terzo. tehrt'soh.	Eleventh Undicesimo. oon-dee-chay'zee-moh.
Fourth Quarto. kwahr'toh.	Twelfth Dodicesimo. doh-dee-chay'zee-moh.
Fifth Quinto. kween'toh.	Twentieth Ventesimo. ven-tay'zee-moh.
Sixth Sesto. sess'toh.	Thirtieth Trentesimo. tren-tay'zee-moh.
Seventh Settimo. set'tee-moh.	Hundredth Centesimo. chen-tay'zee-moh.
Eighth Ottavo. ott-tah voh.	Thousandth Millesimo. mill-lay'zee-moh.

A half, a third, a quarter.	Una metà (un mezzo), un terzo, un quarto.

oo'nah may-tah' (oon med'zoh), oon tehrt'soh, oon kwahr'toh.

Once, twice, three times.	Una volta, due volte, tre volte.

oo'nah voll'tah, doo'ay voll'tay, tray voll'tay.

Number ——.	Numero ——.

noo'may-roh.

MONEY

The monetary unit in Italy is the lira (lee'rah), *which contains* 100 *centesimi* (chen-tay'zee-mee). *The following notes and coins are in circulation:*

NOTES : 10,000 lire, 5,000 lire, 1,000 lire, 500 lire, 100 lire, 50 lire, 10 lire, 5 lire, 2 lire, 1 lira.

COINS : 10 lire, 5 lire, 2 lire, 1 lira.

The rate of exchange varies slightly, but is at present (Dec., 1955) about 1730 lire to the pound.

SWISS MONEY

The basis of coinage in Switzerland is the Swiss franc (100 centimes).

WEIGHTS AND MEASURES

Weights and measures are based on the decimal metric system.

LENGTH

1 centimetro = $\frac{2}{5}$ in. (approx.)
    chen-tee'may-troh.

1 metro = 100 cm. = 39 in. (approx.)
    may'troh.

1 chilometro (Km.) — 1,000 m. = $\frac{5}{8}$ mile (approx.)
    kee-loh'may-troh.

1 in. = $2\frac{1}{2}$ cm. (approx.)
1 ft. = 30 cm. (approx.)
1 yd. = 90 cm. (approx.)

WEIGHT

1 grammo = $15\frac{1}{2}$ grains (approx.)
    grahm'moh.

1 ettogrammo (etto) = 100 g. = $3\frac{1}{2}$ oz. (approx.)
    et'toh (-grahm'moh).

1 chilogrammo (chilo.) (Kg.) = 1,000 g. = 2 lb. 3 oz.
    kee'loh (-grahm'moh).   (approx.)

1 oz. = 28 g. (approx.) 1 cwt. = 50·800 Kg.
1 lb. = 453 g. (approx.) 1 ton = 1,016 Kg.

CAPACITY (LIQUIDS)

1 litro (l.) = $1\frac{3}{4}$ pints (approx.)
    lee'troh.

1 pint	= 0.568 l.
1 quart	= 1.136 l.
1 gallon	= $4\frac{1}{2}$ l. (approx.)

What is the weight of —? | Qual'è il peso di—— ?

kwah-lay' eel pay'zoh dee . . . ?

The length, the breadth. | La lunghezza, la larghezza.

lah loong-ghet'sah, lah lahr-ghet'sah.

The height, the depth, the thickness. | L'altezza, la profondità, lo spessore.

lahl-tet'sah, lah proh-fon-dee-tah', loh spess-sor'ray.

Width (of piece goods). | Altezza.

ahl-tet'sah.

How wide is —— ? | Quanto è alto —— ?

kwahn'toh ay ahl'toh . . . ?

It is ten metres long by four metres broad. | E' lungo dieci metri e largo quattro.

ay loong'goh dee-ay'chee may'tree ay lahr'goh kwaht'troh.

How much per metre ? | Quanto costa al metro ?

kwahn'toh koss'tah ahl may'troh ?

High, tall ; low ; big, small. | Alto, basso ; grande, piccolo.

ahl'toh, bahs'soh ; grahn'day, peek'koh-loh.

TIME

Time is officially reckoned in 24 hours (e.g., 21.30 = 9.30 p.m.), but the older form of reckoning is still used in conversation

What time is it ? | Che ora è? Che ore sono?

kay or'rah ay ? kay or'ray soh'noh ?

It is one o'clock. | E' l'una (il tocco).

ay loo'nah (eel tock'koh).

It is two (three, etc.) o'clock. | Sono le due (le tre, etc.).

soh'noh lay doo'ay (lay tray . . .).

It is half past (a quarter past) five. | Sono le cinque e mezzo (e un quarto).

soh'noh lay cheeng'kway ay med'zoh (ay'oon kwahr'toh).

| It is a quarter to six. | Sono le sei meno un quarto (sono le cinque e tre quarti). |

soh'noh lay say'ee may'noh oon kwahr'toh (lay cheeng'kway ay tray kwahr'tee).

| Ten past four. | Le quattro e dieci (minuti). |

lay kwaht'troh ay dee-ay'chee (mee-noo'tee).

| (It is) ten to nine. | (Sono) le nove meno dieci. (Dieci minuti alle nove.) |

(soh'noh) lay noh'vay may'noh dee-ay'chee (dee-ay'chee mee-noo'tee ahl'lay noh'vay).

| Late, early. | Tardi, presto. |

tahr'dee, press'toh.

| Day, night. | Giorno, notte. |

jorr'noh, not'tay.

| Noon, midnight. | Mezzogiorno, mezzanotte. |

med-zoh-jorr'noh, med-zah-not'tay.

| Morning, afternoon, evening. | Mattino, pomeriggio, sera. |

maht-tee'noh, poh-may-reed'joh, say'rah.

| To-day, to-morrow, yesterday. | Oggi, domani, ieri. |

od'jee, doh-mah'nee, ee-ay'ree.

| This morning, evening. | Stamane, stasera. |

stah-mah'nay, stah-say'rah.

| Last night, to-night. | Stanotte. |

stah-not'tay.

| The day before yesterday. | Ieri l'altro. |

ee-ay'ree lahl'troh.

| The day after to-morrow. | Domani l'altro. |

doh-mah'nee lahl'troh.

DAYS OF THE WEEK[1]

| Monday, Tuesday, Wednesday. | lunedì, martedì, mercoledì. |

loo-nay-dee', mahr-tay-dee', mehr-koh-lay-dee'.

| Thursday, Friday, Saturday. | giovedì, venerdì, sabato. |

joh-vay-dee', vay-nehr-dee', sah'bah-toh.

| Sunday. | domenica. |

doh-may'nee-kah.

| The week. | La settimana. |

lah set-tee-mah'nah.

| Last week, next week. | La settimana scorsa, la prossima settimana. |

lah set-tee-mah'nah skorr'sah, lah pross'sée-mah set-tee-mah'nah.

| Christmas, New Year's Day. | Natale, Capodanno. |

nah-tah'lay, kah-poh-dahn'noh.

| Easter, Whitsuntide. | Pasqua, Pentecoste. |

pah'skwah, pen-tay-koss'tay.

MONTHS[2] AND SEASONS

| January, February, March. | gennaio, febbraio, marzo. |

jen-nah'yoh, feb-brah'yoh, mahrt'soh.

| April, May, June. | aprile, maggio, giugno. |

ah-pree'lay, mahd'joh, joon'yoh.

| July, August, September. | luglio, agosto, settembre. |

lool'yoh, ah-goss'toh, sett-tem'bray.

| October, November, December. | ottobre, novembre, dicembre. |

ott-toh'bray, noh-vem'bray, dee-chem'bray.

| Winter, Spring. | Inverno, primavera. |

in-vehr'noh, pree-mah-vay'rah.

[1] *The names of the days of the week are written with small letters in Italian.*

[2] *Names of months are written with small letters in Italian.*

Summer, Autumn. | Estate, autunno.
ess-tah'tay, ow-toon'noh.

The 1st of March. | Il primo marzo.
eel pree'moh mahrt'soh.

The 25th of April. | Il venticinque[1] aprile.
eel ven-tee-cheeng'kway ah-pree'lay.

I arrived on Monday, May 5th. | Sono arrivato lunedì, il cinque maggio.
soh'noh ahr-ree-vah'toh loo-nay-dee', eel cheeng'kway mahd'joh.

I am leaving on August 11. | Parto l'undici agosto.
pahr'toh loon'dee-chee ah-goss'toh.

I shall return on June 20. | Tornerò il venti giugno.
torr-nay-roh' eel ven'tee joon'yoh.

WEATHER

What is the weather like? | Che tempo fa?
kay tem'poh fah?

It is fine. It is cloudy. | È bello. E' nuvolo.
ay bell'loh, ay noo'voh-loh.

It is raining. It is snowing. | Piove. Nevica.
pee-oh'vay. nay'vee-kah.

It is pouring. | Piove a dirotto.
pee-oh'vay ah dee-rott'toh.

I am afraid it will rain to-day. | Temo che pioverà oggi.
tay'moh kay pee-oh-vay-rah'od'jee.

The fog, the clouds. | La nebbia, le nuvole.
lah neb'bee-ah, lay noo'voh-lay.

Lightning. Thunder. | Lampo. Tuono.
lahm'poh. too-oh'noh.

I hope it will be fine to-morrow. | Spero che farà bel tempo domani.
spay'roh kay fah-rah' bell tem'poh doh-mah'nee.

What is the temperature? | Quanti gradi abbiamo?
kwahn'tee grah'dee ahb-bee-ah'moh?

[1] *With the exception of the 1st (il primo, eel pree'moh), the date of the month is expressed with the cardinal numbers in Italian.*

Is it cold outside ? | Fa freddo fuori ?
fah fred'doh foo-or'ree ?

It is freezingly cold. | Si gela.
see jay'lah.

It is terribly hot. | Fa un caldo terribile.
fah oon kahl'doh tehr-ree'bee-lay.

The sun, the moon, the | Il sole, la luna, le stelle.
stars.
eel soh'lay, lah loo'nah, lay stell'lay.

PLACES OF INTEREST

Only a few of the more important are listed below.

TURIN (TORINO)

Il Duomo (the Cathedral).
eel doo-oh'moh.

Palazzo Madama.
pah-laht'soh mah-dah'mah.

[*This contains the famous Cappella della Santissima Sindone* (kapp-pell'lah dell'lah sahn-tees'see-mah seen'doh-nay), *in which is preserved a part of the linen cloth in which the body of our Lord was wrapt after the Crucifixion.*]

La Pinecoteca (art gallery).
lah pee-nay-koh-tay'kah.

L'Armeria.
lahr-may-ree'ah.

Il Museo di Antichità.
eel moo-zay'oh dee ahn-tee-kee-tah'.

Il Parco del Valentino (public gardens).
eel pahr'koh dell vah-len-tee'noh.

Environs : Superga ; Stupinigi.
soo-pehr'gah ; stoo-pee-nee'jee.

MILAN (MILANO)

Il Duomo (the Cathedral).
eel doo-oh'moh.

Brera (art gallery).
  bray'rah.

Il Castello Sforzesco.
  eel kah-stell'loh sforrt-sess'koh.

Sant 'Ambrogio (Romanesque basilica).
  sahnt ahm-broh'joh.

**Santa Maria delle Grazie (with Leonardo da Vinci's
  " Last Supper ").**
  sahn'tah mah-ree'ah dell'lay graht'see-ay.

La Scala (famous opera-house).
  lah skah'lah.
    Environs : La Certosa di Pavia (famous Carthusian
      monastery).
      lah chehr-toh'zah dee pah-vee'ah.

VENICE (VENEZIA)

Piazza S. Marco.
  pee-aht'sah sahn mahr'koh.

La Basilica di S. Marco (St. Mark's).
  lah bah-zee'lee-kah dee sahn mahr'koh.

Il Palazzo Ducale (The Doges' Palace).
  eel pah-laht'soh doo-kah'lay.

Il Canal Grande.
  eel kah-nahl'grahn'day.

L'Accademia di Belle Arti (art gallery).
  lahk-kah-day'mee-ah dee bell'lay ahr'tee.

Cà d'Oro (museum).
  kah dor'roh.

Palazzo Pesaro (modern art gallery).
  pah-laht'soh pay'zah-roh.

Ponte dei Sospiri (Bridge of Sighs).
  pon'tay day'ee soss-pee'ree.

Ponte di Rialto.
  pon'tay dee ree-ahl'toh.

SS. Giovanni e Paolo.
  sahn'tee joh-vahn'nee ay pah'oh-loh.

S. Maria dei Frari (containing Titian's
" Assumption ").
sahn'tah mah-ree'ah day'ee frah'ree.

S. Giorgio Maggiore.
sahn jorr'joh mahd-jor'ray.

Environs : Il Lido (summer resort) ; Murano
(famous for the Venetian glass industry) ;
Burano (where Venetian lace is made) ; Torcello
(an island with an ancient cathedral).
eel lee'doh ; moo-rah'noh ; boo-rah'noh ; torr-chell'loh.

GENOA (GENOVA)

La Cattedrale (the cathedral).
lah kaht-tay-drah'lay.

Palazzo Ducale (containing the civic museum).
pah-laht'soh doo-kah'lay.

L'Annunziata.
lahn-noont-see-ah'tah.

Il Porto (the Harbour).
eel porr'toh.

Environs : Nervi ; Pegli ; Portofino (all charming
sea-side resorts).
nerr'vee ; payl'yee ; porr-toh-fee'noh.

FLORENCE (FIRENZE)

*Florence is beautiful at all seasons of the year, but the most
interesting time to visit it is during the spring Musical Festival
(Il Maggio Musicale, eel mahd'joh moo-zee-kah'lay), which
has much in common with the Edinburgh Festival.*

Il Duomo (the Cathedral).
eel doo-oh'moh.

Il Battistero (the Baptistery, with its famous Golden
Doors).
eel baht-tee-stay'roh.

Il Bargello (the National Museum).
eel bahr-jell'loh.

Palazzo della Signoria.
pah-laht'soh dell'lah seen-yor-ree'ah.

Galleria degli Uffizi.
gahl-lay-ree'ah dayl'yee oof-feet'see.

Palazzo Pitti.
pah-laht'soh pit'tee.

Boboli (park) ; Le Cascine (park).
boh'boh-lee ; lay kah-shee'nay.

S. Croce (containing the monuments of many great Italians, and wonderful frescoes).
sahn'tah kroh'chay.

S. Maria Novella (the Dominican basilica, with magnificent frescoes).
sahn'tah mah-ree'ah noh-vell'lah.

San Marco (the adjoining convent is fitted up as a museum, especially famous for the frescoes of Beato Angelico).
sahn mahr'koh.

San Lorenzo (with the Medici chapels).
sahn loh-rent'soh.

Palazzo Riccardi (with wonderful frescoes by Benozzo Gozzoli).
pah-laht'soh rick-kahr'dee.

Environs : Viale dei Colli (a wonderful drive, with enchanting views) ; Fiesole ; S. Miniato al Monte (famous for its mosaics) ; Certosa del Galluzzo (a monastery, famous for its liqueurs).
vee-ah'lay day'ee koll'lee ; fee-ay'zoh-lay ; sahn mee-nee-ah'toh ahl mon'tay ; chehr-toh'zah dell gahl-loot'soh.

PISA

Il Duomo ; La Torre pendente (the Cathedral ; the Leaning Tower).
eel doo-oh'moh ; lah torr'ray pen-den'tay.

Il Campo Santo (monumental cemetery).
eel kahm'poh sahn'toh.

ROME (ROMA)

Il Foro Romano (the Forum).
  eel for'roh roh-mah'noh.

Il Palatino (the Palatine, with remains of ancient
  buildings).
  eel pah-lah-tee'noh.

S. Maria degli Angeli.
  sahn'tah mah-ree'ah dayl'yee ahn'jay-lee.

Il Pantheon (the only ancient edifice in Rome which
  is still in perfect preservation).
  eel pahn'tay-on.

Il Colosseo (the Colosseum).
  eel koh-loss-say'oh.

Il Campidoglio (the Capitol).
  eel kahm-pee-dohl'yoh.

Le Catacombe di S. Callisto (catacombs of St. Callixtus).
  lay kah-tah-kom'bay dee sahn kahl-lee'stoh.

La Basilica di S. Pietro (St. Peter's).
  lah bah-zee'lee-kah dee sahn pee-ay'troh.

Il Vaticano.
  eel vah-tee-kah'noh.

I Musei Vaticani (the Vatican museum).
  ee moo-zay'ee vah-tee-kah'nee.

Il Castello di Sant' Angelo (fortress).
  eel kah-stell'loh dee sahn-tahn'jay-loh.

Piazza del Popolo.
  pee-aht'sah dell poh'poh-loh.

Piazza Navona (Circo Agonale).
  pee-aht'sah nah-voh'nah (cheerr'koh ah-goh-nah'lay).

S. Maria d'Aracoeli.
  sahn'tah mah-ree'ah dah-rah-chay'lee.

S. Maria Maggiore (the largest of the eighty churches
  in Rome dedicated to the Virgin).
  sahn'tah mah-ree'ah mahd-jor'ray.

S. Giovanni in Laterano.
  sahn joh-vahn'nee in lah-tay-rah'noh.

La Via Appia antica (the Appian way).
  lah vee'ah ahp'pee-ah ahn-tee'kah.

Le Terme di Caracalla (Baths of Caracalla).
   lay tehr'may dee kah-rah-kahl'lah.
Pincio ; Villa Borghese (parks).
   peen'choh, vill'lah borr-gay'zay.
Il Gianicolo (Janiculum).
   eel jah-nee'koh-loh.
Il Quirinale (Quirinal).
   eel kwee-ree-nah'lay.
S. Paolo fuori le Mura.
   sahn pah'oh loh foo-or'ree lay moo'rah.

The names listed on pages 109-110 suggest only a small fraction of the sights worth seeing in Rome. Almost every street contains something of interest to the visitor, and in particular the numerous fountains with which the city is adorned are well worth careful study.

   Environs : Frascati ; Tivoli ; Villa d'Este ; Abbazia
      delle Tre Fontane ; Lago di Nemi.
         frah-skah'tee, tee'voh-lee, vill'lah dess'tay, ahb-baht'
         see-ah dell'lay tray fon-tah'nay, lah'goh dee nay'mee.

NAPLES (NAPOLI)

Il Duomo (S. Gennaro) (Cathedral of St. Januarius).
   eel doo-oh'moh (sahn jen-nah'roh).
S. Chiara.
   sahn'tah kee-ah'rah.
**L'Acquario (the aquarium : one of the finest in
   Europe).**
   lahk-kwah'ree-oh.
Palazzo Reale.
   pah-laht'soh ray-ah'lay.
Museo Nazionale.
   moo-zay'oh naht-see-oh-nah'lay.
Palazzo di Capodimonte.
   pah-laht'soh dee kah-poh-dee-mon'tay.

   Environs: Posillipo ; Vesuvio ; Pompei ; Sorrento ;
      Capri ; Grotta Azzurra.
         poh-zeel'lee-poh ; vay-zoo'vee-oh;
         pom-pay'ee ; sor-ren'toh;
         kah'pree; grot'tah ahd-zoor'rah.

PALERMO

La Cattedrale (Cathedral).
    kaht-tay-drah'lay.

Museo Nazionale.
    moo-zay'oh naht-see-oh-nah'lay.

**Il Palazzo Reale (The Royal Palace. It contains the
    Cappella Palatina, *kahp-pell'lah pah-lah-tee'nah*,
    a gem of mediaeval art).**
    eel pah-laht'soh ray-ah'lay.

**S. Giovanni degli Eremiti (St. John of the Hermits,
    one of the earliest existing Norman churches).**
    sahn joh-vahn'nee dayl'yee ay-ray-meet'tee.

Orto Botanico (Botanic Gardens).
    or'toh boh-tah'nee-koh.

Villa Giulia (Flora) (park).
    vill'lah jool'yah (flor'rah).

    Environs: **Convento dei Cappuccini (Capuchin
        Convent, in the subterranean corridors of
        which are preserved mummified bodies).
        Monreale (Cathedral).**
        kon-ven'toh day'ee kahp-pooch-chee'nee.   mon-ray-
        ah'lay.

*Lack of space has made it impossible to do more than mention
a very few of the monuments or places of interest which await
the visitor to Italy, but there is hardly a single town of any size
in the country which does not deserve a visit from all lovers of
art. This is particularly true of Tuscany, where the smaller
cities, such as Siena and Lucca, contain priceless art treasures
and are equally worth visiting for the sake of the natural beauties
amid which they stand.*

INDICE ALFABETICO

Le parole stampate in maiuscolo si riferiscono ai capitoli, in cui l'argomento é trattato diffusamente.

INDEX

The words printed in capitals refer to Sections, in which the subject is dealt with at length.

ITALY

C. Muro

6988

Solenzara

Sartène

p.to Vecchio

Bonifacio

Strait of Bonifacio

C. Testa Maddalena

Caprera

ROME

Ostia

Lido di Roma

Colonia Marina

Anxio

Asinara

G. of Asinara

p.to Torres

Terranova

Tempio

Golfo Aranci

Tavolara

Pontin

I.

Sassari

Chilivani

Oziéri

C. Carcio

Alghero

C. Marargia

Mᵗ Limbara

4459

Mᵗ Lerno

3589

Mᵗ Alto

3697

Siniscola

C. Comino

C. Mannu

Bosa

Nuoro

Macomer

3445

Gavoi

Orosei

G. of Orosei

TYRRHEN

SARDINIA

Gennargentu 6017

Aritzo

Oristano

G. of Oristano

Laconi

Séui

Tortoli

Laconsei

Ales

Ivili

Nurri

Jerzu

Terralba

Mandas

S. Gavino

Guspini

Sanluri

Senorbi

C. Pecora

Villacidro

Siliqua

Decimomannu

Monastir

3507

Muravera

Quartu S. Elena

SEA

Iglesias

Carbonia

Sestadi

Cagliari

Carloforte

S. Pietro

S. Antioco

Teulada

Pula

C. Carbonara

G. of Cagliari

C. Spérone

C. Teulada

C. Spartivento

MEDITERRAN

C. S. Vito

38

Ægades Iˢ Trapani Pᵗ

Marettimo

Favignana

C. Boeo

Marsala

Masara

C. Granitola

La Galite

C. Serrat

Ferryville

C. Blanc

Bizerta

E A N

G. of Bone

La Calle

Tabarka

Matuir

La Marsa

Gulf of Tunis

C. Bon

Kelibia

ALGERIA

Randon

Téboursouk

Téboursa

La Goulette

Carthage

Menzel-Temimi

Menzel bon Zelfa

Grombalia

Nabeul

Pantelleria

Souk-el-Arba

Béja

Medjerda

Medjez-el-Bab

Zaghouan

Ghardimaou

TUNISIA

Souk-Ahras

Le Kef

Enfidaville

Hammamet

Gulf of

Hammamet

8

10

12

Lon